David Doernberg

## *About the Editor*

PETER TERZIAN has written for the *New York Times*, the *Los Angeles Times Book Review, Newsday*, the *National*, Slate.com, *The Believer, Bookforum, Columbia Journalism Review*, and *Print*. He lives in Brooklyn, New York.

# HEAVY
# ROTATION

# HEAVY ROTATION

## TWENTY WRITERS ON THE ALBUMS THAT CHANGED THEIR LIVES

### EDITED BY PETER TERZIAN

HARPER  PERENNIAL

NEW YORK • LONDON • TORONTO • SYDNEY • NEW DELHI • AUCKLAND

HARPER ● PERENNIAL

FIRST EDITION

*Designed by Aline C. Pace*

Library of Congress Cataloging-in-Publication Data is available upon re-
quest.

ISBN 978-0-06-157974-5

09 10 11 12 13   OV/RRD   10 9 8 7 6 5 4 3 2 1

# CONTENTS

# INTRODUCTION

PETER TERZIAN

It took me years to figure out music. I was an only child, with no savvy brother or sister to guide me through what seemed like a confusing, arcane world of bands, songs, logos, and discographies. I entered high school in 1981, and heard my classmates talking about *Abacab* and *2112* and *Live at Budokan*. They may as well have been speaking in Finnish. But I had no great desire to be led out of my ignorance. Every afternoon, I boarded the school bus for home, finding a seat somewhere in the middle, not too far back (where the "burnouts" sat) and not too far in the front (where the girls sat). The doors slapped shut. From behind me I could hear a boom box clicking into action, and what I later learned were the opening bars of AC/DC's "Hell's Bells" or Led Zeppelin's "Immigrant Song," loud and terrifying, wailed over our heads. The bus driver scolded and threatened ineffectually. The volume was turned higher. Music, I thought, is a bad, bad thing.

At least, this kind of music, teenager music, was bad. At home, I still listened to the soft rock of the previous decade: Olivia Newton-John, Kenny Rogers, Anne Murray. I found that music could be a solace for the muddle of school life. Not playing music: I took piano lessons, and I was a dismal, nonpracticing failure. Listening to music, though, got me daydreaming. I would create stories or imaginary films based on the lyrics of whatever song was playing on my record player, or I would fantasize that I was cast as the star of a musical set at my school, with scenes where the whole lunchroom burst into choral accompaniment, dancing on the tables, while I crooned in the spotlight. Still, I was aware that my favorite music was dated and wimpy. If anyone asked what bands or singers I liked, I said that I didn't listen to music. Better to appear hopelessly out of touch than to carry a torch for a kind of music so ripe for ridicule.

At some point, a leaflet arrived in the mail stating that our local cable company was adding some new stations. One of them was MTV. Soon I was spending afternoons on the living room couch, one leg hooked over the armrest, watching video after video. The heretofore mysterious world of popular music began to reveal itself. In the early '80s, new bands were sprouting up like gaudy wildflowers. British people sang in bright, flapping clothes, plinking out notes on electronic keyboards; hair grew in every color and direction. My classmates talked about the videos they'd seen: "Karma Chameleon," by Culture Club and Boy

George, a man who wore a dress; "Rio," by Duran Duran, who made the girls swoon; "When Doves Cry," by Prince, who left us all aroused and perplexed. There was something for everyone, even me. I made a mental list of my new favorites: Squeeze, the Police, and Men at Work.

I began to buy records. In time, I had amassed a small but respectable music collection. By my senior year, I was in possession of my father's old brown Ford sedan and a driver's license, and I was a regular customer at Strawberries, the local chain record store. But it was by an egregious sidestepping of copyright laws that I learned the most about rock music. In downtown Albany, a fifteen-minute drive from my house in the suburbs, there was a dumpy basement shop run by a grizzled man who often had food in his beard. The racks were filled with unwrapped albums, both current titles and classics. You could buy one of these already-played records for seven dollars. Return it within three days—enough time to tape it—and you got four dollars back. Blank cassettes were displayed prominently by the cash register. The message was clear. My friend Doug and I would drive to Music Miser after school, and I would "rent" albums in pairs, filling blank tapes with crackly recordings made on my Sears all-in-one stereo.

It was like learning a new language with a hundred different dialects. I could now discuss bands in the school hallway with confidence, debate who was cool and who wasn't, argue over best and worst albums. I wrote song lyrics on my blue cloth binder. I went to my first concert, the Pretenders and Simple Minds, with three friends and no supervising adults at the nearby Saratoga Performing Arts Center, an outdoor arena with a lawn where people drank beer and smoked pot. The drinking and smoking seemed wrong—that way lay rowdiness and chaos—and I felt a little uncomfortable being out so late in the night, away from home. But the music had saved me from ignominy, and I was grateful.

Still, listening to record albums offered me more than mastery of my social world. Around the same time, I became interested in good literature and in what we then called "art" movies. I read Italo Calvino and Philip Roth, and discovered François Truffaut and Jim Jarmusch, and the world beyond our suburb began to seem a little bit larger. At the same time, books, movies, and records made my insides seem a little bit larger too. I sat in my room, in front of my turntable, on warm summer afternoons when I really should have been outside, my parents said, getting some fresh air. (There was a new refrain in our house: "Turn the music down.") I played my records over and over again. I listened very closely, and sometimes the songs seemed to be written about me, for me. How did all of the hyper, hiccuppy tracks on the Buzzcocks' *Singles Going Steady* manage to neatly sync up with the twisting, mutating emotions induced by my high school crushes? What was the strange excitement that swept over me when I listened to Patti Smith's *Horses*, sex rising like incense from my stereo?

At other times, the songs and words seemed to have nothing to do with my life. What, for example, could a suburban adolescent male possibly take away from Joni Mitchell's *Hejira*, an album about a woman entering her thirties, wrestling with the alternating calls of freedom and commitment as she travels into the heartland, meeting lovers and drifters, frequenting jazz clubs and staying in lonely motel rooms? And yet, somewhere, deep inside me, it felt like a window was being opened. I was learning about what it meant to be an adult, about the many different ways of living a life.

Almost as soon as I began to like music, I began to like music writing. I became a compulsive reader of record reviews, racing to the magazine rack whenever I went to the record store and leafing through *Rolling Stone*'s back pages to memorize the star ratings. (Later, I threw over *Rolling Stone* for the much hipper *Spin*, which introduced me to the sharper, smarty-pants style of music writing that prevails today.)

In college and the years after, I got deeper into fiction and poetry, and soon I had two loves, literature and pop music. It seemed that never the twain would meet. I couldn't listen to music while reading or writing, and vice versa. Each seemed to have different rules of engagement, to occupy a different quarter of my brain. Sometimes I got snobby and thought that I had outgrown pop music, that from now on I was going to walk in the loftier air of the republic of letters. But of course music kept drawing me back. My visits to bookstores were divided between the long, twisting rows of fiction and the meager bay devoted to music books. I would think about how few novels and poems and memoirs of literary quality had been written about pop music, and how rarely music criticism provided the emotional heft of contemporary fiction.

I came up with the idea for the book that you now hold in your hands for selfish reasons—I wanted to bring music and literature together. The truth is that writers love music. A good ear is almost a requirement of the job; the best writing has voice, has rhythm. When writers get together, the first question that they ask each other is, "What have you been working on?" The second is often, "What have you been listening to?"

I've long suspected that I was not the only one whom music shook to the very core—not the only teenager sitting on the floor of his room, with his ear bent toward the stereo speaker, hanging on to every note. I wanted to learn about other listeners, other record collections, other emotions and responses. I wanted to read about the ways in which life and music make contact, get tangled up. And so I invited a handful of contemporary writers to share their musical histories and passions, to tell us about the albums that moved them or inspired them or brought them back from the edge.

And in how many different ways, in how many cultures and countries, have these writers listened. Through Walkman headphones, on an evening stroll past the bright lights of Broadway, come tales of flying cowboys and rodeo girls. From a pirated cassette purchased in a northern Indian railway settlement, the marital trials of four Swedes unfold. Over a car tape deck, on a biting cold Mississippi night, the ghostly words of a near-forgotten blues artist reveal themselves. In the pages that follow, you'll read about a Toronto girl whose drive to share her obsession with a curly-haired cartoon orphan leads her to sing on a local television station; about a New Jersey teenager who finds a surrogate father in a shy Beatle; and about two Seattle moms whose world of baby dates and pediatric appointments is transformed by a glam-rock drag queen. In each case, a beloved record album becomes a portal to another world—a world not only bigger, sexier, and sometimes scarier but also wildly interesting and impossibly alluring.

# HEAVY ROTATION

## STILL ILL

The Smiths: *The Queen Is Dead* (Sire Records, 1986)
### Benjamin Kunkel

**Rosalind. They say you are a melancholy fellow.**
**Jaques. I am so. I do love it better than laughing.**

—from *As You Like It*

I must have been a child—logic insists on it, and snapshots show proof—but I retain hardly any sense of subjective continuity between then and now, and whenever I allude to the boy I was I feel slightly dishonest, as if I'm pretending to a personal acquaintance with someone I don't actually know. Few of my boyish interests have survived, and even when it comes to, for instance, our family's dogs, the Denver Broncos, and girls, at the time, far more has changed than has remained the same. Nothing, then, in my present incarnation seems to date from any earlier period than when I first found myself flipping my cassette of *The Queen Is Dead* back over to the A-side the moment the last, weird strains of "Some Girls Are Bigger Than Others" had faded out, and returning once more to the album's opening song and title track. A hearty British woman's voice, sampled from an old film, leads a chorus of "Take Me Back to Dear Old Blighty"; the apparently patriotic number is rudely dispatched by a peal of feedback; a murderous rhythm is set up on unaccompanied drums; the guitar begins woozily to wah-wah; a brushed cymbal shivers; the mean-spirited funk of the bass line kicks in; you hear that moan you'd recognize anywhere; the first moaned word is "farewell"; everything I feel in the way of snottiness, shyness, and distraught longing stands ready to be recognized by the ten unaccountably angry and joyous tracks before me; and, with that, I am tempted to say, my life as I know it begins.

In 1986 I was living with my family in the humdrum town of Eagle, Colorado. I had just become a teenager and was applying to prep schools in New England. I considered myself a rather tragic, intelligent, and solitary figure, and was accordingly full of fantasies of escape from the baffled cows and squinting hicks who swelled my middle school class. At the same time there was obviously something wrong with me, a basic temperamental deficiency that prevented me from taking life with that casualness, amounting almost to grace, displayed by normal people. Suicide or fame seemed likely destinies. Meanwhile I had picked up a bad case of Anglophilia; in one egregious instance, when I and a friend DJ'ed a middle school dance I delivered my patter in what I took to be a British accent. Prep school, in my imagination, which is to say my ignorance, was a waiting congregation of superior youth rather than the hothouse of class distinctions it would prove. Does it go without saying that I had as little sense of humor as a dog? If someone slipped and fell I thought this was funny but otherwise couldn't find a reason to laugh.

The songs on the radio said nothing to me about my life. And as the elder brother of two sisters I had no one to induct me into the mysteries of sophisticated music for teenagers. My method was to choose a band, almost at random, from the "college" chart at the back of *Rolling Stone*, and to buy the band's latest tape whenever I could get to a record store; the nearest was thirty miles away. One challenge with parents who themselves grew up on rock and roll is the difficulty in scandalizing them with your own tastes, and it's clear to me now that the bands I selected from the college charts were those whose names suggested my parents might find their music offensive or at least bewildering. The appeal of the Smiths' name came from the strangely arrogant declaration of commonness, and I liked the punkish implication of regicide in the title *The Queen Is Dead*. That went "God Save the Queen" one better, without implying, as listening to the Sex Pistols would have done, that I harbored any intention of ever having sex.

My method was a risky one. The Screaming Blue Messiahs, for instance, had a name satisfactorily suggestive of madness and violence, but I found I didn't really like their music. With the Smiths I got lucky. The folky tastes I'd picked up from my parents allowed me to take right away to the bright acoustic texture of Johnny Marr's arrangements, which then conveyed me into an atmosphere far removed from any '60s-ish mood of barefoot good health and slack openheartedness. Both side-opening tracks, "The Queen Is Dead" and "Bigmouth Strikes Again," were surging anthems of destruction, spiteful in their very rhythms; and even where the music itself was not in the least rebarbative, inflected instead by jazz or rockabilly or West African highlife playing (strains my ear identified long years before I could name them), Morrissey remained at all times an obnoxious vocalist. Most exciting, maybe, was his way of boasting of his inadequacies. When he broke into the palace on the title track and the Queen said, *Yes, I know you and you cannot sing,* he replied in his unpleasantest voice: *That's nothing, you should hear me play piano.*

The Smiths were the first contemporary band I encountered that enabled the all-important act of identification with the singer. No one could touch Morrissey for literateness and melancholy, and if I knew anything at the time it was that I too wanted to write and was unhappy, woebegone, that is, in the trackless way of early adolescence, where I couldn't see how I had ever come into this condition or might ever get out. And then there was the more curious fact, according to *Rolling Stone,* that in a literal sense no one could touch Morrissey. This witty, famous, and in my opinion handsome man was a self-proclaimed celibate with no interest in sex. His superiority was his sadness, his sadness his solitude, and his solitude his martyrdom. He was too good for this world, or at least for famously miserable Manchester, never mind the bypassed cow town of Eagle, Colorado, where every household appliance was like a new science, and all that happened in high school was the girls got pregnant and the boys got trucks.

May I admit that my headlong identification with handsome Morrissey was enabled by another circumstance? Now at thirty-five I begin to have the face I deserve, and already in high school it was clear I was not to be a tall man, but in middle school things were different. After having been a boy ignored by girls, suddenly I was fending off requests to "go" with them; and when away games and tournaments took us to other schools (I was a starting linebacker on the football team, a benchwarmer at basketball, and a very erratic wrestler), more girls petitioned me with folded notes containing phone numbers. This change was a boon, since being attractive, if you're feckless and morose, can substitute for actual activity, and permits you, above all, to feel that your isolation from the human race owes as much to your rejecting it as to its rejecting you. In practical terms, however, I had no idea what to do with my looks besides trade them for the opportunity to get my hands on some mammary glands. And yet when I succeeded for the first time in effecting this momentous transaction I learned that tits, to the touch, were no different from regular skin, like you'd find on someone's ankle or belly.

With male classmates, things weren't much better, since as a boy without a sense of humor I felt ill at ease and almost foreign among them. When the friends I would soon abandon for prep school came over, I never played the Smiths; this was music for listening to alone while you lay in awe on your bedroom floor. And there would have been equally little sense in admitting that in emulation of Morrissey I'd adopted a program of celibacy—a commitment I couldn't explain or, probably, should an opportunity present itself, uphold. In general, the phenomenon of other people was a matter of polite endurance while I waited to resume my self-contemplation. I was especially uncertain whether to class my traits as virtues or defects, and for this state of narcissistic suspension the Smiths were the perfect soundtrack. Already I must have apprehended that Morrissey's words, for all their eloquence, possessed the supplemental eloquence of meaning the exact opposite of what they said. Because in truth he *liked* to be alone. He *wanted* to be unlovable. Which didn't really mean he was—it just meant he didn't want to know if he was or not. The problem with other people is that ultimately they have to decide what they think of you and how much time they'd like to spend in your company—whereas you, being stuck with yourself, are spared the necessity of such conclusions.

Before long, I had added to my Smiths collection the eponymous first album, as well as *Meat Is Murder*, on which my favorite track was "That Joke Isn't Funny Anymore." Best of all, though, was *Louder than Bombs*.

Bought at a mall in Denver on a trip with my family, this stupendous compilation of singles and B-sides remains one of the happiest purchases of my life: twenty-four songs that I'd never even known existed! It was all but unbearable to sit in the backseat of the car reading the lyric sheet during the long drive back to Eagle—but there could be no question of asking my parents to play the tape.

Up to then they'd listened to even the worst of my music with curiosity or at least without complaint. They'd never protested the heavy metal affectations of Def Leppard or Ronnie James Dio's forays into satanic imagery, never mind the soggy lugubriousness of Dennis DeYoung, former lead vocalist of Styx and the living low point of my prepubescent tastes. And once I graduated from the Top 40 to the college charts, they were similarly unperturbed by the fuzz and churn of Hüsker Dü or the nasal nonsense of R.E.M.'s Michael Stipe. Ruinous tolerance of the baby boomers! In fact my father helpfully explained that R.E.M. meant rapid eye movement—*I* know, *Dad*—and that Hüsker Dü was a memory game played by Norwegians. But the Smiths my parents could not abide. Morrissey's voice on the living room stereo seemed to cause my mother genuine physical distress—*The moaning,* she said, in pain, *the droning, the monotone*—and more than once she'd insisted that I put on something, anything else. It was great: I felt credentialed as a teenager. And in this way I duplicated the Smiths' own discovery, namely that if there is one adolescent attitude more insufferable than the punk rock sneer, it's that combination of superiority and self-pity best expressed by Morrissey.

While beneath the abject vocals runs—most perverse of all!—a current of delight.

I liked to think of myself as miserable at the time, and can't have been completely wrong about this. But I believe that as I plotted my escape from home and from rural idiocy, and contemplated the vocation of poetry, I was happier than I knew or could say. I was becoming someone I might enjoy knowing, for all that the ineluctable sorrow of the poetic personality would forever remain my cross to bear. And in listening to the Smiths now, as I've never stopped doing for long, I detect an analogy to this smuggled cargo of enjoyment—because it isn't really, though it can seem so, that Morrissey's miserabilist lyrics and freestyle moaning have nothing in common with Johnny Marr's jangling, joyous music. It's more nearly the case that the music supplies the secret truth of the words, an occult gladness at their heart.

All skill is joyful, said Yeats—and it's worth remembering that the Smiths were not only a great band but also a very good one. Johnny Marr in particular was a guitar savant, and the band became expert around him. Born John Maher, he met Steven Morrissey for the first time at a Patti Smith show in 1979, but once the two formed a band, three years later, it was too late for punk, and anyway Marr's fingerpicking virtuosity and magpie tastes in music caused him to scorn any three-chord cloddishness. All that remained of punk for the Smiths was a chary attitude toward guitar solos (never indulged till the final album), a DIY approach to business matters that ultimately proved their undoing, and one more musical idiom to exploit at will. It was typical of Marr to conceive of a chord progression (for "The Headmaster Ritual") as, in his words, what Joni Mitchell "would have done had she been an MC5 fan or a punk rocker." A similar cool lucidity, uncanny in a teenager, marked the way he recruited Morrissey: "I wanted someone who was just a singer and wasn't playing an instrument. I didn't want a musical cowriter. I wanted someone who looked good and was serious about words. But most of all, I wanted someone who was as serious about it as a life option as I was."

Marr and Andy Rourke, the band's bassist, had been in a funk outfit before the Smiths, and Rourke's twirling "song-within-a-song" bass lines (as Marr called them), played at the high end of his instrument's range, made for a lot of the Smiths' distinctive sound, while the melodic work they did freed up Marr's guitars for blooming chromatic excursions. The only real primitive in the Smiths, from a musical standpoint, was the drummer Mike Joyce, late of the Manchester punk band Victim, and after the Smiths' initial recording sessions exposed his limitations, he set about diversifying his attack. Before long he was capable of shimmering high-hat dazzlement as well as a tom-tom fusillade or glam-rock stomp. And it seems to me that the Smiths' music, considered apart from Morrissey's words, often carries through from major to minor chord and back again a mood of continuous pleasure gained from the realization of one's gifts.

The instrument-playing Smiths were all thrillingly young (Morrissey being four years their senior) when the band formed; Johnny Marr was just eighteen and would only be twenty-three when they broke up. And note something else: each of the four band members was a first-generation Englishman and the son of economic migrants from Ireland. Surely among the things you can hear the band forging in the smithy of its sound are the tools of release from the constrictions of immigrant life. "A rush and a push and the land that we stand on is ours," sang Morrissey, adapting an old Republican slogan to the purposes of a conquest in reverse. The Smiths were in their own eyes a tremendous, historic band much deserving of popularity—Morrissey was notably obsessed with their position on the UK singles chart—and they knew they might get what they wanted.

Still, the question remains of what the bright, glad music of Johnny Marr and the rhythm section has to do with Morrissey's ill-humored words and off-key moaning. After all, Morrissey couldn't read music or play an instrument and often recorded his vocal only after the rest of the track was completed. And when you first listen to a song like "Heaven Knows I'm Miserable Now" it can seem that the Smiths are afflicted with as extreme a case of what you might call *words/ music dualism* as anything the most riven Cartesian could suffer by way of a mind/body split, or else why should such a maundering recitation of self-pitying complaint be laid down atop a piece of music virtually simpering with felicity? I couldn't have answered the question at age fourteen, but then I doubt I would have loved Morrissey so much at the time if I hadn't detected at a level beyond words—the level, precisely, of music—that he too was having a good time.

The apparent paradox is that while Morrissey complains of his clumsiness and sorrow and self-doubt, the music that backs him up is deft, assured, and often simply happy. There's irony there, of course, but the deeper and more interesting thing is identity: despondency and exultation made one. The closeness of Morrissey's vocal lines to Marr's and Rourke's melodies tends to produce the impression that the *words* have summoned the music, rather than the other way around. Listen again to the songs, and notice how when Morrissey wonders how you can stay with a fat girl who'll say *would you like to marry me? and if you like you can buy the ring?* and when he says that the story of his life is that he was once sixteen, clumsy, and shy, you can hear melancholy making a deal with happiness. The deal is off the books but unconcealed.

Melancholy, after all, can act as happiness's enforcer. Sadness can serve as a pretext—one is often useful—for saying I can't go out tonight (*I haven't got a stitch to wear*) and I'm not the man you think I am (*I'm sorrow's native son*) and, no, I've never had a job (*because I'm too shy!*). So tell the people at the threshold to your room that, alas, you must stay inside to mope. Then shut the door and rejoice: solitude is the only intimacy that's not intrusion. Besides, alone again you can work on your lyrics about the pathos of being alone.

I arrived at St. Paul's School in the fall of 1987. One of the few decorations I brought for my room was a Smiths poster, and the first time I left campus I went straight to the record store and purchased a copy of the just-released *Strangeways, Here We Come*. It would have been a happier occasion if *Rolling Stone* wasn't reporting that the Smiths had split up.

My mourning of the Smiths was complicated by actually listening to *Strangeways*. The use of synthesizers offended my teenage puritanism and, more than that, Morrissey's lyrics had now vaulted so far over the top that even I could detect a hint of camp. I understood that "Unhappy Birthday" and "Girlfriend in a Coma" were humorous compositions, but didn't see what was so funny—everything I felt was still too near the bone and too close to home. Nevertheless my fandom, my fidelity, were still enough that the first short story I wrote in high school was called, after the majestic cut off *The Queen Is Dead*, "There Is a Light That Never Goes Out": a piece of teenage gothic, all pallor and doom and trickling blood, with—I think so anyway—a shovelful of soil falling over the main character's head.

The next year I roomed with a preppy kid from Darien, Connecticut. He had a bowl haircut, played soccer, and favored the Allman Brothers. One day in early September, I returned to our double to find that my poster of Morrissey, Marr, Rourke, and Joyce standing outside the Salford Lads Club, the poster I'd tacked proudly to the wall, now hung *inside* my school-issued armoire, behind my shirts and jackets. When I asked why this was, my roommate replied that he wasn't into Euro-fag music. I took the poster down and rolled it up, lest we be suspected of sucking each other's dicks and putting product in our hair. Soon CD players arrived to overwhelm the age of cassettes, and since all I had of the Smiths were tapes, the band became a private indulgence, Walkman listening. By this time—I was fifteen—I'd realized that I might not be cut out for celibacy. But in my laziness and unhappiness and general unsuitability for life, I still thrilled to the words "I decree today that life is simply taking and not giving, England is mine, it owes me a living." All the anti-work songs in the Smiths' canon nourished my ambition of never having a real job and becoming a writer instead. Sex, after all, only takes a few minutes—but with a job they make you work all day.

I've never gotten over the Smiths. In fact, just when it seemed I would have to give them up, because life had begun to wring occasional concessions of joy from me, I got the Smiths back again. Throughout high school the human capacity for laughter had remained a solemn mystery to me, and I can remember each of the three times, over four years, when I deliberately said something funny. But once I went to college and began to unlock the secrets of comedy and irony, once I perceived at last that you could exaggerate things and understate them and didn't always have to speak in deadly earnest, I realized what anyone else could have told you right away: the Smiths are hilarious! Morrissey—he's joking. He means it but he's also joking. And that feeling of pleasure running underneath the lyrics of the songs? It's in part the pleasure of being witty. Ah-ha: it's *arch*.

The final twist was that the excuse of comedy gave all the old feelings a new justification. Even up to today I have managed to conceal from myself, with the help of this music, the exact proportions in which I am melancholy and amused, superior and timid, glad of my solitude and afflicted by it. For going on twenty-two years now, more time than it takes to raise a kid and send him to college and buy him a drink, I have been playing the Smiths on heavy rotation. For more than two decades I've been able to think, about any number of abortive romances, *I know it's over, and it never really began, but in my heart it was so real....* I can never get over the gamboling bass line of "Cemetry Gates" or the opening guitar riff and first cracking drumbeat of "Girl Afraid." And even such throwaway details of production as the children's choir singing "hang the DJ" on "Panic" and the sample from an old hypnotism record on "Rubber Ring" are things that I love. Almost none of the Smiths' songs, in my experience, has proved easily outgrown, and it occurs to me that I'm still sorry the band broke up, while my own breakups I've always recovered from quickly enough. Not that I haven't followed Morrissey's solo career, but when a great singer and a great band part ways, the future songs of the singer are always diminished, even if his solo work is musically every bit as good as his work with the group. This is because it gives words a special power to receive the loud, implicit endorsement of the entire band in whose name the singer is singing. The solo artist, like everyone else, only speaks for himself.

# WHAT ANNIE KNEW

*Annie* Soundtrack (Columbia Pictures Records, 1982)

## Sheila Heti

**W**hen I was five years old, my eyes were clouded to my childhood duties by the peak fan experience of my life. It was 1982, and everything was Annie. I developed a new-to-me, curious sensation of both wanting to be like her and believing myself to be already more like her than anyone else could possibly be—a certainty about kinship of soul that is the mark of devotion. For nearly a year I moved through the streets of my neighborhood with this feeling inside me.

My parents obligingly took me to see the movie three times. I begged for and received on my birthday a furry, plush Sandy doll—Annie's dog. For two years running I dressed as Annie on Halloween, wearing my usual clothes and a clown wig—not quite Annie, but close. I called my mother (who had curly red hair like Annie) my "Annie-mom," which she hated, but I wouldn't stop. At the time, I loved Annie more than I loved my own mother. And like any romantic obsession, wherever one looks, there is the beloved.

But though I called my mom "Annie-mom," there was something wrong with the term. She was *not* my mom, after all. For I was an orphan like Annie. I longed to be in an orphanage. One afternoon, I demanded to be shown my birth certificate to determine my true parentage. Which turned out to be my parents.

My dreams falling short, I would sit on the windowsill (which was not wide like Annie's windowsill in the orphanage, so not that easy to sit on) and gaze out the window—not at the dirty streets of New York as Annie did, but at my neighbor's middle-class home across the road. I'd sing the song "Maybe" in the heartbroken way that Annie had, a lament for what my real parents might be doing at that moment—not downstairs but perhaps in Pittsburgh. "He may be pouring her coffee / She may be straightening his tie . . ."

I wanted the replica Annie locket but never got it. But since this was the age before VCRs were common, my parents bought me the record, which became my constant companion. I would put it on the living room stereo and dance around, singing along, or sit still with it cradled in my arms and imagine I was she, the object of my admiration and my twin. I had never before seen a girl portrayed who had so many feelings and yet was so gutsy.

The album cover was beautiful, too. It was white and unfolded to reveal stills from the film: Annie hanging off an open bridge; Annie laughing beneath a pile of silk sheets; Annie smiling up at Daddy Warbucks, holding his hand—two lost and lonely souls who found each other and were "together at last, together forever." I would gaze at these pictures like they were portals to a better, more glamorous world.

It was one of those dreary Sundays when I had to do chores all morning, and I got through the cleaning by singing the song that Annie and the orphans sang as they poured soapy water down the stairs of the orphanage: "It's the hard-knock life for us. . . ." If there was one thing my mother liked less than being called "Annie-mom," it was me vacuuming while singing loudly and self-pityingly, "Santa Claus we never see / Santa Claus, what's that! Who's he?" Especially since we were Jews.

Once the house shined like the top of the Chrysler Building, I lay on the rug in the TV room and turned on the set to watch *Big Top Talent*, a popular variety show in Ontario at that time. It was hosted by an unfunny clown who stood in the center ring of a circus, and to the applause and appreciation of the crowd sitting in bleachers that seemed to rise all the way to the heavens, he'd introduce, one after another, local singing or dancing or singing-and-dancing troupes—children as small as three years old in matching tutus, or grown-up kids of twelve or thirteen in glittering black costumes dancing awkward jazz routines. It was definitely my favorite show.

Really, I was fascinated by any show in which kids my age (or usually a little older) got to dance and sing and josh around, for nothing looked more fun or more glamorous than being a child star. I'm not sure whether I became obsessed with Annie because I was already craving to be a child star, or if my obsession with Annie made me want to be a star and live in a mansion with Daddy Warbucks and sing all my feelings. In any case, Annie was really so lucky: not only was she Annie, but she got to *play* Annie on the big screen.

Sitting, watching, I felt a desperate need to join those kids on the TV and sing a song from *Annie*. And I determined I would. I imagined myself singing in the center of the big top. I would choose the perfect song, and I would bring Annie to the masses. (I didn't quite realize, of course, that not only were the masses sick of Annie, but that it was the masses that had brought Annie to *me*.)

Happily enough, my father was one of those kind and obliging parents whom any bossy child is lucky to get. He agreed to take me to Kitchener-Waterloo, a dreary town several hours west of Toronto, so I could go on TV and sing "Tomorrow." Not that this was my favorite track on the album, but it was the one that best captured Annie in her hard-done but optimistic essence. My favorite song was "You're Never Fully Dressed Without a Smile":

*Hey, hobo man! Hey, Dapper Dan!*
*You both got your style*
*But brother, you're never fully dressed*
*Without a smile!*

"Tomorrow," on the other hand, had more heart. It was the song Annie would sing to herself when she felt sad and lonely in the orphanage, to remind herself that though she was *stuck with a day that's gray and lonely*—I could relate to that—she couldn't give in to sadness, but rather had to *stick out her chin, and grin, and say, oh, the sun will come out tomorrow.* She sang this not only in the orphanage but also in the White House with Franklin Delano Roosevelt, as they stood proudly before a portrait of George Washington.

I don't know how my father managed to get me on the program. No doubt he called them up and they were happy to fill a spot on what was probably not as popular a show as I imagined. Though I was already singing "Tomorrow" once a day, I have a recollection of "rehearsing" it, my father crouched at a distance with his hands cupped around one eye as though he were looking through a TV camera.

The only thing I was afraid of now was the crowd; I had to be stronger and have more courage than even Annie. *She* had no audience, while I would be standing in the center of the big top, with its tall bleachers like the ones in the circus I had gone to when I was three, packed with parents and children.

But it would be okay: my father had stood in front of me like a camera and I felt I was prepared.

Early one January morning, my father and my pregnant mother and I drove in our brown Honda to Kitchener-Waterloo and pulled into a half-empty parking lot. I suddenly felt shy and aghast at what I was going to do. Wasn't it enough to love Annie in the privacy of my own home? Did I have to proclaim it on television? But I quickly reminded myself that, yes, I did have to proclaim it on television.

We got out of the car and walked through the front doors of a concrete warehouse, my mother and I parting with my father. We went to the "green room" while my father left us to go shake hands with the clown.

We entered what looked like a classroom, the yellow walls covered with mirrors. The other kids who'd be performing that day were standing around with their mothers, who were less like my mother than any mothers I'd seen. My mom seemed as nervous as I was. She had come from Hungary in her mid-twenties and was still intimidated by Canadian women. And naturally she dressed me all wrong. While the other girls stepped into spandex and sparkles, my mother put me into an ugly, conservative, pinky-beige dress, the same one I'd later be forced to wear for our family portrait.

Shockingly, every mother was putting makeup on her daughter. I was the smallest one there, but even if I had been older, my mother would never have done such a thing. Makeup was for ladies. I pleaded with her that I needed makeup, too. My mother nervously pulled a lipstick from her purse and rubbed a little bit into my cheeks. I felt utterly sad and humiliated.

But the greatest shock was to come. A tall, skinny woman came along to lead me away from my mother. She took my hand and I followed her through the heavy, leaded, double doors of the changing room, into what I still imagined would be a circus tent filled with parents and kids. Instead, we emerged into a cold, barren concrete space. There was the set I knew so well. There were two large cameras, a beaten-up brown piano, and, most depressing of all, an "audience" of five or six empty folding chairs.

I was still trying to take all this in, to reconcile myself to the truth of the situation, when the lady pulled me by the hand to the side of the stage. She picked me up under the arms, plunked me down on a stool, and walked off. On a nearby stool sat a stuffed monkey. The show had already begun. A boy in brown lederhosen was dancing an Irish jig on the set. For some warmth I touched the monkey and it made a loud squeak, and the boy dancing the jig stumbled and looked over. I pretended I hadn't touched the monkey. And even later, on the car ride home, and waking up the next day, and a week after that, I told myself I hadn't touched the monkey.

The set was cleared of the boy, and the clown, dressed in green, took the stage. He was an elderly giant. He waved me over. At this point the camera began taping. I walked onto the set, slowly, looking around like a small cat new to a house, and stood on the large silver star sticker I had seen so many kids stand on before me. I waited there dutifully, looking blankly out at my audience: two or three stage moms smoking and chatting with each other.

"Hello," said the clown.

I didn't reply.

"Your name is . . . Sheila Heti. And what are you going to sing for us?"

"I'm going to sing the song 'Tomorrow,'" I replied, anxious to begin the song, finish it, then get in the car and go home.

"What! You're going to sing the song *tomorrow?*" the clown said, laughing loudly. "Why don't you sing it today?"

I stared at him and blinked expressionlessly, at a loss for words. My nervousness must have been palpable, but also some of my irritation.

"Oh!" he chortled, and clapped his hands together. "You're going to sing the song that's called 'Tomorrow,' but you're going to sing it today!"

I looked over at the brown piano and a horror welled up in me. I realized that I would have no accompaniment to my song, and that it was too late to do anything about it. No one performed without music. But no one in my family had thought of it.

"And who's your singing teacher?" the clown asked.

No one had taught me to sing. I didn't know what to say. Were kids taught to sing? Wasn't that something kids just knew?

"My daddy taught me," I lied.

"Daddies are good teachers all right!"

At last, after what felt like an hour, the clown said: "And here we have . . . Sheila Heti . . . singing the song that's *called* 'Tomorrow,' but singing it today."

Which I did—a bit hurriedly, but full of conviction, unsmiling, tiny, stern:

*The sun will come out . . . tomorrow!*
*Bet your bottom dollar that tomorrow*
*There'll be sun.*
*Just thinking about . . . tomorrow!*
*Clears away the cobwebs and the sorrow*
*Till there's none. . . .*

In the months following my performance on *Big Top Talent*, my relationship with Annie changed hues. I was still an Annie fan, but I really was more of an Annie colleague. Though I was only five and she was ten, I believed that I had a feeling for what she had been through. Having witnessed the guts of showbiz for myself, and been shaken by how radically it contrasted with what I'd imagined, I felt hardened—though not in an entirely bad way. My point of view was bleaker now, less naive. But it was more like Annie's. Life was a scam. It was like the orphans sang on the album: " 'Stead of treated we get tricked / 'Stead of kisses we get kicked / It's the hard-knock life."

The experience pretty much killed any possibility of my idolizing a musical star ever again—and I haven't since. I've tried, but it hasn't taken. Now whenever I find myself in a situation in which I must empathize with the young men of my generation for whom going to see a rock star in concert is an act of devout pilgrimage, I have to go all the way back to when I was five, before my innocence was lost. I've never been able to shake the sense that, while it might appear that, for instance, the White Stripes are performing in a grand stadium to a crowd of screaming fans, in reality they're on some crummy set before some folding chairs in a concrete warehouse in Kitchener-Waterloo.

Several years ago, my father called to let me know that Aileen Quinn—the actress who played Annie—would be in town for one night performing in the musical *Saturday Night Fever*. Did I want to go see it? I wasn't sure. But we hadn't gone together to see a play in years, so I said yes. The show was mediocre, and Aileen Quinn disappointing: she was wearing makeup, and she had breasts.

When the show was over, standing in the lobby, my father began goading me into going backstage to say hi to her. I wasn't sure I wanted to. Seeing her onstage had been enough. I would have nothing to say. She would likely be tired. But I went with him anyway, and together we stood in the back alley beside the stage door.

It was a dark, dismal day, and we huddled in the doorway as the energetic performers slammed their way out, running down the alley through the pouring rain. As it goes in the movies, we were just about to give up—we had been waiting fifteen minutes—when out she came: Aileen Quinn, with a man. He left her at once up the alley, and she stood there blinking at the sky. I had to work to see her as Annie. There was only the slightest resemblance. Naturally, she was no longer a girl of ten.

I said I was sorry to bother her but I just wanted to tell her that I liked her performance—and then I mumbled how I'd once been a great fan of Annie. She thanked me warmly and said she loved playing Annie.

Then my father said, "It's raining. Can we drop you off anywhere?"

I caught my breath. She hesitated a second, then agreed. So there we were, me and my dad and Annie, running through the rain to our car. I got in the back seat where I sat silent, embarrassed and burning, while my dad drove through the gray Toronto streets, chatting amiably with Annie about all the things I had done since I was ten, when it was Annie I loved best. I was as shy as a little girl, and couldn't think of anything to say. My dad and Annie spoke like two grown-ups—she talked about the show and how much she liked being on the road—while I stared at the backs of their heads.

I had always wanted to meet Annie, and imagined it a million ways. I could never have guessed, back when I was little, when it would have meant everything to me, that one day it would happen—but that it would take twenty-one years, and that it would be like this: dropping an unrecognizable woman off at the subway, and watching her run through the pouring rain.

# 3

## THE QUIET ONE

The Beatles: *Meet the Beatles!* (Capitol Records, 1964)
**Alice Elliott Dark**

It's George because, just because, there's really no reason you can say, you just know it's him, he's the one, with his skinny pipe cleaner legs and coconut-shell hair and the way he dips his head so you can't see his eyes, only his eyebrows, he's not like his friends who stare straight at the camera, the way your brother would, your brother always gets lots of attention, he knows how to look your mother straight in the face and make her laugh, whereas you do it wrong, your jokes fall flat, so you've learned to dip your head too; so you understand George; you get him; it's true, even though it doesn't make any sense, you're only a child and he's a famous man millions of miles away; but a lot of things are true that don't make sense, like your father evaporating, your real house empty and dark and about to be sold, you living at your grandparents' where you are now, sitting on the green scratchy rug in the den watching the Beatles in their first performance on *The Ed Sullivan Show*. Your brother is pointing to Paul and saying he's John and you tell him he's wrong, it's the other way around, but he's a know-it-all and doesn't believe you and what can you do but wait and hope the truth will out somehow, this is what you've learned to do, to wait, because people don't listen when you speak, they see right through you and around you and over you and it has been that way for as long as you can remember, ever since that day on the beach when you were maybe eighteen months old and you were sitting on the sand looking out at the lighted ocean and you were thinking, you were right in the middle of a thought when your father swooped down like a seagull and snatched you up and you tried to tell him no, no, you wanted to stay just where you were, your legs burning on the hot sand, because you were having the first real and important thought of your life and you wanted to finish it; but then your father plucked you from the earth and lifted you up. He smelled of Coppertone. You heard him breathe, not quietly like most people but louder, like a waterfall, his skin on yours was electric and soothing, and you felt a little faint and lay your head on his shoulder and he pulled you tighter and closer and your thoughts rose up into the sky until you didn't see them anymore and you were just a part of him. Attached. You saw into him and felt who he was, and how could you ever explain it, it wasn't a word or a sentence of a narrative, it wasn't logical, it was a rolling sphere of tiny particles, maybe as small as atoms, that were held together by a physical force, so that the whole mass made sense only as a sum of its parts. You understood him. Even when he was about to disappear you knew. You look at George. Later they'll call him "the shy Beatle" but he's not shy, you can tell, it's something else that keeps him from lifting his eyes to the camera; it's the rolling sphere inside him; and you love him. You love him! You remain sitting on the rug but you have left the room and you are with him, walking on a hill, the grass is full of daffodils, he is holding your hand and you are his . . . sister. His beloved little sister. He loves you as much as a father would, he is going to look after you now, everything is going to be all right. You hardly even care that your brother is proved wrong about John and Paul and that your other brother and sister jeer at him and he gets angry and runs from the room and slams the door, and you feel an impulse to look at your mother to see what she's going to do about it but what's the point of looking at her, you already know she's going to say it's harder on a boy, boys need their fathers more than girls do, so you decide to forget about it and stay with George. He needs you now. You go to bed thinking of him and soon your father appears at your ceiling, he's done this every night recently, he hovers like a helium balloon, he comes in his work suit and his tie hangs straight down toward you like a tongue, and he asks you what you did that day, a moment you've liked up until now because you're getting to see him far more often than you have since he and your mother separated three years ago. After that you weren't allowed to talk to him all week, only on Friday, the night you stayed with him, you were forbidden anything more, your mother caught you sneaking a call once and ripped the phone out of the wall. Now you have what you've wanted, to talk to him every day; you've felt so full of pity for him; every night you've pictured him coming home tired from work where he saved people—sometimes children!—by cutting open their chests and fixing their hearts, a really hard job, you've pictured him pulling into the driveway exhausted, putting his key into the lock of a completely dark house, opening the door and walking in all alone. All alone. This is better, having him come to your room every night to talk, he's here with you now. But on this night, when he asks you about your day, you don't want to tell him, you don't want him to know you love another person aside from him, another man, and so soon, he only went away a couple of weeks ago, and you try to hide it from him, you want to protect your own heart from being operated on by your father, you don't want him to see the new growth that has taken root, because it would make him sad, and he was already too sad, he died of sadness . . . except he isn't dead, he's here at your ceiling, searching your face, he sees you and he understands what you're thinking, and you usually love this, it's what you've always wanted, but suddenly you also want a private space in your mind, you want to be with George without your father knowing, you want it both because you don't want to hurt his feelings and because

George is yours, you don't want to hear what you father has to say about him. You turn over to hide your face. Like Eve, you think, running from God. You are Eve and Ed Sullivan is the snake and George is the tree of knowledge, or something like that, you try to think it through, but sleep snatches your mind away, it plucks you up, and soon you don't exist. Then you do again, it's morning, and you and your brother beg your mother to take you to the store so you can buy *Meet the Beatles!* It came out recently, around the time your father went away, but you haven't gotten it yet because everything is weird and you haven't been out much except school and when you do go out you're surrounded by silence, even if everyone's laughing and trying to cheer you up it's silent, silent, everywhere, like when one of the mothers drives right by your real house on the way back from school and no one in the car says anything, not a word, about your father, it's like he doesn't exist, never had, even your mother says nothing, nobody does, nobody, not a soul. But George will talk about him, you just know it; George understands he's only away on a trip, he's in the South Seas, on a beach in Tahiti like the one in *Mutiny on the Bounty*, which happens to be one of you and your father's favorite movies; and your father looks like Marlon Brando, his mouth does, and his profile, and what's in his eyes. George can help you remember your father is in the South Seas operating on people there who have bad hearts, he's fixing them up, but he can still come to your ceiling at night, he can do both, he's free now. You're tempted to tell your mother this

THE QUIET ONE 31

because she cried when the phone rang in the middle of the night at your grandparents' house, she ran downstairs and answered it and you followed her and saw her crying, even though they were divorced, you didn't understand why she cried but you saw her do it and maybe she'd like to know he was really okay; but she's standing at the sink with her hands in soapy water and you hear her mutter something hard to herself in the same tone she used when she said he worked too much, never marry a doctor, they think they're God; so you simply wait to hear whether or not she'll take you to the record store. You and your brother each want your own copy of *Meet the Beatles!* but your mother says that's ridiculous and a waste of money, you can perfectly well share, but you have your own money, all those coins you'd been saving up to buy a horse; you'd worked hard for *years* setting the table and sweeping the driveway and weeding the garden and every night you spilled the coins out of the jar painted with flowers with a latch on the top and they came out smelling of iron, like the water in Cape May, and you counted the money again even if you hadn't made any more since the night before and you wrote down how much you had on a pad of paper; and then you read your book about how to take care of a horse, you memorized the parts of a hoof and the names of the grooming tools—dandy brush, curry comb, hoof pick, mane comb—and how to use them, move the curry comb in circles, be very gentle with the hoof pick so as not to cut the frog, which is in the center of the hoof and will hurt if you scrape it, you don't want to do that, you'll be gentle with your horse; or you would have been if you hadn't realized on the night your father was eclipsed that it would take you years of chores to save enough dimes and quarters to buy a real horse and it would never happen in your childhood, ever. You'd realized this as you lay in bed that night two weeks ago, waiting to hear what you'd known since he called that afternoon and told you not to come over that day, he had a cold; you knew that wasn't true, that it was something else, and whatever it was meant you'd never hear his voice again, and when you got off the phone you went to the kitchen and told your mother that you and your brother weren't going that night because your father was going to die, and she told you that was silly. She wasn't listening. Your father hadn't listened either when, the weekend before, you told him everything was going to be all right and that you were never going to have a friend over again when you went to visit him, you were only going to be with him; no more best friend, no more second best friend, no more girl across the street whom you and your father had walked home through thick sparkling snowdrifts, no more running around in the yard at night with a dozen kids chasing fireflies and placing them in jars to put on the chest next to the bed as a nightlight, running and panting while he stayed in the real house den with a glass of brown liquid in his hand, his bare legs poking out of a pair of madras shorts, his veins round and tight as the stems of a hosta, full of liquid, ugly from standing long hours in the operating room, you'd never leave him alone again while you had a choice; he should listen to that; he should absorb it into his veins; he should hear you. He had not. He had not. I'll buy my own record, you tell your mother, I have my own money, and she shrugs. After school she drives all four of you to the store and you and your brother rush to the bins and each grab an album and you look at the pictures and there he is, George, his face familiar, known to you in a visceral way, and you clutch your record to you and when you get home you write your name on it in large letters, in Magic Marker, indelible, so everyone will know not to touch it, it's yours alone. You don't yet have a record player of your own so you have to listen downstairs in the living room on your grandparents' old Victrola and your brother fights for his record to be the one listened to, and that's okay with you because yours will last longer that way (it has lasted; you still have it; it still plays), and as you listen you look at the pictures over and over again and you read the liner notes and you feel like you do at recess when you lie on the ground and two of your friends stand at your head and feet and pull your arms and legs in opposite directions and stretch you long and longer; and then you listen some more. Each time the record finishes you start it again. And when your mother says "dinner" and you go into the kitchen to eat the songs are still in your head and they stay there, they go up the stairs to bed with you, when your father appears at your ceiling that night you tell him about this new music, this new feeling; and you hope he understands. He may; he was a musician when he was a boy, you have a picture of him from a newspaper saying he was a child prodigy; in time, he may understand. Every night you tell him about the music, and every day you listen to the record, and every time you do it makes you glad; and sad too. Sad because of the yearning in the Beatles' voices, a longing you feel inside yourself but you never hear in the voice of any person you actually know. Sad because as you listen to the Beatles' desires and love and pining you ache too, and in that ache there's a part of you that knows the truth, that no matter how many letters he writes you from the South Seas, or how regularly he comes to your ceiling, your father really is dead and you'll never see him again, ever, not even in heaven, because there's no such heaven where living people stay just as they were, he told you that, and that there is no Santa Claus; you'll never see him again. And no matter how many times you walk around town with George or how close he sits while you're doing your homework or how often he picks you up from school you know he's really very far away, in another country. But there's another part of you that puts all that aside and listens anyway, searches for his voice within the harmony, searches for his guitar line, his lead; all you have to do is find the beginning and then it's like pulling a thread, the whole song unravels; you have him, just him, all to yourself. He goes to camp with you that summer, he stays in the infirmary with you when you are so homesick you can't eat, homesick not for your new stepfather's house where your room is tiny and miles away from your mother, but for your real house, your old life, your living father. George sits in the chair by your sickbed at camp and talks to you when you have no energy to do anything but look out the window at the pines with the light coming through them like angel light if only there were a heaven; George talks to you about everything you've done together and everything you will do, he tells you how he really likes John but Paul bugs him, Paul's bossy, he tells you about his mother and the house where he grew up, he tells you how much you mean to him and how pretty you are in spite of the braces and the bad haircut, and you promise him you'll never leave, you'll never go to a friend's house when you can be with him, and he says not to worry about that, he's going to be busy sometimes so you are allowed to have fun while he is. You say you'll think about it. Finally you get a postcard from your mother and that makes you feel better, less alone, and you eat a little food and then a little more until you're strong enough to get up and go back to your cabin and you get in a canoe and George has never tried canoeing before but the other girls know Beatle songs and you all sing them while you paddle around the lake and George is embarrassed when everyone sings the song he sings, "Don't Bother Me"; and while they're singing you talk to him quietly and tell him you like it, you love it, it thrills you, it scares you, like the time your father came home from work and found you and your brother arguing and he grabbed you and dragged you upstairs by the arm and he beat you and you just lay there while it was happening until he remembered who you were and who he was and he ran from the room and you lay on the bed looking at the ceiling until he came back in and his face loomed over you and his tie hung down so close you could have bitten it and he told you he was sorry, he was sorry, and you said it was okay, you understood, he had a hard job, too many people wanted too much from him, everyone thought he could save their life and he couldn't always do it, he had patients who died, children died, he wasn't a god. You tell George this as you drift around the lake, and then more about him, too, lots of stuff; and George asks you where your father is and you don't exactly know, maybe Tahiti, but somewhere, still alive, and George nods; and when you get back to your stepfather's house he's still somewhere else; no one ever speaks of him. Then three years later, your relationship with George is beginning to change a little, he's growing out of being your brother and is starting to *like*-like you; and you're beginning to write stories and poems and take photographs and draw while you listen to more and more Beatles records; you still parse the songs, searching for him, you take them apart as you always have but now you put them back together again and you see how his part fit into the whole and you realize art isn't one thing but many layers and textures and sounds and feelings, and truths, many truths. One day you're sitting with your friend Todd among the ancient rocks at the end of your stepfather's driveway and it's spring so the daffodils are everywhere, hundreds of them, and you're talking about music and records because he plays the guitar, he plays lead; he looks you right in the face in a way no one else has, and he asks you the question that no one else does: *what's it like to have a dead father?* And you feel him seeing into you, he sees a rolling sphere, and suddenly you're just you alone, no George, no father, just you and him sitting among the daffodils on a rock, and you think, my father's dead? And then you think, oh, yeah, he is, he is; and you remember everything; and you understand; that your father's life was made up of lots of musics, leads and bass and rhythms, and so would yours be; and that the whole of him was more than his death, and so are you; and you look at this beautiful boy sitting in front of you and he's still looking at you, he's waiting, he's listening; and you say, *it's weird,* and he gets it.

# WHAT YOU'VE DONE TO MY WORLD

4

Fugazi: *Fugazi* (Dischord Records, 1988)

Mark Greif

**G**enres of music ought to be classified by the emotions they inspire in their listeners. Joy, comfort, arousal, self-satisfaction—for rock music, those are emotions it's easy to talk about.

Punk rock began for me with fear. The music arrived for me historically late, at the end of the 1980s, and personally early, when I was fourteen years old. I was a child. Rock is for children. You have to be that young to feel it with full intensity, to hear the drumbeat strike and think it is the world reaching out to punch you. With experience the nerves become sclerotic, and you learn that the promises of the lyrics are lies and posturing. By twenty-eight you're left with the knowledge that you're the fan of a deficient art form. Your emotions have evolved to deny you rock music's best benefits, and it's become much too late to develop any comparably deep feeling from any other music. As a grown-up, still listening to the same stuff, you're genuinely ruined.

At fourteen I just knew I wanted to be ruined. Punk promised physical violence, a buzzing charge, like the wish that someone would hit you in the face. I desperately wanted the feeling of violence in my life, without the reality. There may be a personal mystery, of *why* this is what I wanted; or a social mystery, of why I seem not to have been completely alone in my desire, judging from the way other people approach rock and punk. Behind it is a bigger, more interesting mystery: how music, with the lyrics put to one side, can manage to contain "violence."

Only heavy metal had promised anything comparable to punk up to that point in my life. But gratifying as I found the double bass–drum kick and guitar speed of Metallica or Megadeth, I could never find myself, my own conflicts, inside metal's war-and-lunacy lyrics. I felt more at home in lyrics from the golden age of what's now called "post-punk," the eccentric independent-label music after punk that turned back from insults to society, to a hatred of oneself.

Punk and post-punk seemed to offer violence against the listener by the band and singer, and then violence against everybody else by the band and singer and listener all together. The lyrics often seemed aware that they couldn't come up to the music, or that they only gained whatever power they had from the music behind them. They could be comic-aggressive, or they could be pathetic. In choruses like "Fuck school fuck school fuck my school / What's the matter, buddy? Fuck you!" (the Replacements) or "I'm a leper . . . / Who should I believe? / Safest to wallow in my own esteem" (Dinosaur Jr.), you had the two lyrical poles of the songs I loved. But the music itself was neither comic nor pathetic. It was threatening, exhilarating. It let me lie in bed at night with the lights off, headphones on, in a state of genuine, crushing fear.

How do you explain this for the benefit of someone who has never pursued these feelings? You might have to swing the telescope around and let him see magnified the tiny dots of a whole archipelago of sociological facts about that child in bed: white kid, suburbs, middle-class, petted in school, bored, helpless, angry for no explicable reason. I would rather say, maybe too simply, that it was just something about fourteen, when you are old enough and strong enough to be capable of adult acts, and young enough and baffled enough to be totally incapable of accomplishing them, and thus you are a raging superman when listening alone to your Walkman and still a frustrated and thwarted child in real life. Anyway, that was fourteen for me.

There were varieties of mayhem in the music, and I became a connoisseur. Listening to early British punk, I made judgments about those first bands from the end of the '70s. The Sex Pistols offered nihilistic, careless, unspecific violence ("No future / No future for you!"). This meant little to me, and knowing nothing about them but what I heard on record I felt the

Sex Pistols were slick, overproduced, and boring; I left that tape alone. The Clash, who had images of police riots lithographed on their record covers, were great, and delivered songs of militant resistance, like "The Guns of Brixton"—and it's true that, while I rode the bus to school, I used to sing to myself: "When they kick at your front door, how you gonna come / With your hands on your head, or on the trigger of your gun?" But I also felt ashamed. I had a weirdly strong reality principle about certain things and by that age I had worked out a worldview that said that if the police kicked down my door, I would be a victim, not a freedom fighter. Straight to the concentration camp I would go. It was hard to sing along with songs that so obviously represented other people's power fantasies, especially when they didn't believe that they were fantasizing. Yet I didn't want to have to live with my own weakness, unexpressed, every day. That meant finding a fantasized violence that also acknowledged it was fantasy—the comic side of punk, again.

I fell in love with the Damned, from that generation of the inventors of punk. They spat on me in the right way, by which I mean neither cynically (like the Sex Pistols) nor over-earnestly (like the Clash), but for the sake of the fact that I was enjoying listening to them. And then the band and I were going to get together and fucking spit on everybody else! The Damned had produced these Grand Guignol visions of ridicule ("She can't afford no cannon / She can't afford no gun at all") and superpower ("I was born to kill") and insults to their fans waiting outside the stage door ("Standing in the pissing rain / Must be a drag") and then out-and-out cowardly murder ("Stab your back! / Stab your back! / Stab your back!"), and I loved them for it. The lyrics were bolted firmly to the music, which was so fast and so trebly (especially on the bad second-generation tape of an LP that a French-Canadian bunkmate gave me at summer camp) and so gloriously painful to listen to, that the absurd violence in the words matched a real musical violence—which, as I've suggested, is the connection that's powerful in punk, that's interesting, that scares.

In my early teen years, in those waning years of post-punk, listening to recorded music weighed about equally, at school, with attending weekend shows. (Nobody called these "concerts.") People passed around cassette tapes of new music at the progressive, which is to say weird, high school I attended after years in public school—a sudden switch for me from Cat Stevens and the Steve Miller Band to Hüsker Dü and the Jean-Paul Sartre Experience. And there was at least a little real violence to be had at shows, which was always a topic of interest. On Mondays at school, you'd hear reports of shows that had taken place over the weekend in which some stranger might have been hurt, pushed to the ground, bloodied by an elbow or a fist; and you'd hear what your friends had had to do with this, what they saw. Or if you'd gone out, well, then you had been there yourself, you'd heard rumors, or you knew. I never personally saw anyone badly hurt at a show, but there was always a kind of hope. I remember a concert at an ice rink, too big to be a real "show," and therefore more dangerous, because there were college frat kids who didn't abide by the semi-protocols of the weekend all-ages punk events, where at least if you knocked someone down you would put out a hand to pick him up. At this event, someone was reputed to have broken a leg, or his back, and been taken out on a stretcher; and a friend fought his way to return from the very front delighted with this news—"There's blood on the floor! There's blood on the floor!" In fact, blood could always flow because a head might accidentally fly into a nose in the late form of slam-dancing known as moshing. Moshers gathered together tightly, at the center of a circle, hurling themselves at each other, bouncing off shoulders, thrust out to the periphery and pushed back in again by waiting hands, flinging themselves at wherever the mass was thickest, in what was called the "pit," and this was safe—I participated in this myself, warily. Or within the pit men faced off, sometimes just in pairs, sometimes even with a single sweat-soaked young man waiting for a challenger, and that scared me again.

One of the most thriving punk subgenres of my era was called "hardcore," a music especially suited to moshing, and that was one of the genres with which my musical life restarted when I was fourteen. I was following up an immoderate prepubescent diet of Woodstock-era "classic rock," the suddenly execrable music of mothers and fathers. Hardcore was awesome.

It, too, was scary, because of the ultrafast repetitive drumbeat, the shouted lyrics, the chopped-up guitar, but also, at least initially, because of the shaved-headed culture surrounding the music. Shaved-heads meant skinheads to the child that I was, and skinheads in the 1980s meant neo-Nazis, young German and English Hitler-fancying hooligans who ran wild in the streets of Bremen or Leeds; National Front brutes, racists—the sort of people you watched *60 Minutes* segments about with your parents, back then, in the embarrassment of the family unit. In between classes at school it was explained to me by my peers that not all hardcore was skinhead and that anyway there were antiracist skinheads, although there *was* racist white supremacist hardcore, too, in England especially, but that was hard to find and . . . I was dubious. It seemed to me an unhealthy fixation, this focus on which shaved heads were Nazis and which were not. Why not just have hair? I was told about a world called "straight edge," a subculture of shaved-headed (or crew-cut) hardcore punks who not only were antiracist but additionally forswore drugs, alcohol, and tobacco (though not violence), and Magic-Markered Xs on the backs of their hands in imitation of the policy punk clubs employed to keep underage drinkers from the bar. I didn't really care; I didn't Magic-Marker any Xs on my hands. Assorted band cassettes came and went, and at some point my friend Becky K. gave me a tape of the complete works of the great, defunct D.C. hardcore band Minor Threat. Now, to that recording, I responded;

I listened, stunned, and with very little idea what to make of it. When I run through it in memory—I'm certain that I haven't played it in at least fifteen years—I always think of some lyrics from "Out of Step":

*Don't—smoke*
*I don't—drink*
*I don't—fuck*
*At least I can—fucking think!*

I should add that Minor Threat lyrics were bellowed, as if at someone, ultraloud, with churning chords underneath. I didn't smoke, drink, or fuck either—I looked forward to all three, but it wasn't working out. It was evident that the people in the straight-edge world were radically unlike me, trying to get away from things I didn't need to get away from. Most of the music I knew from those classic rock radio stations had a habit of inviting you in, colluding with you in the feeling that you could belong, could take the standpoint of the singer. When Mick Jagger sings to get off of his cloud, you know he's not talking to you, he's addressing *some other person*—basically it's a song for you to sing along with. Much of punk was like this, too—a shifting river of bile that would run up against you for a moment, maybe, but then flow downstream to somebody else. Whereas if Ian MacKaye of Minor Threat told me to get off of his cloud, I knew I should get off. It wasn't my cloud. I felt this all by means I didn't understand entirely—in part by the tense regimentation of the music, in part by the stern expressions in the songs, not to mention the intensity of their strange subculture. Minor Threat managed to exclude me totally, and I responded to this with curiosity.

The gap became a little too wide for me, I thought, with the song "Guilty of Being White," which shouted about the pain and rage of being guilty, simply by being white, for all previous white generations' crimes. It seemed to fulfill the suspicion that hardcore and its shaved-headed practitioners were racist after all. I brought this up with Becky K. when I returned the cassette.

"Becky, like . . . they're 'guilty of being white.' But aren't they . . . trying to get out of their guilt? They're, like, really mad about it?"

Did I mention that Becky K., also fourteen, was pierced, ultraleftist, and always way ahead of me? Her eyes started, from behind round spectacles, with perhaps the most perfect look of contempt I had received to that point in high school. I knew that I had exposed myself as inadequately punk.

"*No,*" she said. "They are totally guilty of being white. That's the whole thing. They're dead serious. They *are* guilty. We're *all* guilty."

Well, I knew I was guilty already. I was guilty of being white, just as I was guilty of being male, guilty of not being poor, guilty of being straight, guilty of everything that a good politically progressive kid could be guilty of. But Minor Threat managed something impressive: to make me feel really outside of their world, rejected by them, *and* at the same time guilty, reminded of forms of personal rottenness I could do nothing about, of which I *knew* I ought to remind myself more often. Here was something new: the violent rage and alternating hatred and self-hatred of other punk, but with some really good social reasons for hating yourself. This was a use of musical violence even the self-censuring and responsible part of me could get behind.

The other record I remember from when I was fourteen that scared and alienated me in the same way as the Minor Threat album was Public Enemy's *It Takes a Nation of Millions to Hold Us Back*. I wasn't black, Public Enemy didn't want me, and the music had the same dual effect of righteous thrills and a sense of complete non-belonging. (That album, too, reminded you that white people ought to be hated.) Even today I wish there were more records, everywhere, that obstruct the identification process of rock, that teach more listeners not to identify. You don't deserve it sometimes, and maybe singers should forbid it. This was a valuable piece of education for me. Not all feelings produced by art belong to you—even if in some measure only your own response brings them into being. Sometimes art-emotions have to be sequestered, moved into a different category of response, to free you to be a responsible human being: someone, that is, who knows to stand at a remove and appreciate others, while acknowledging that they don't want you, they don't care if you're there.

Punk held all the satisfactions of starting violence in its music and then channeling or directing it by its lyrics—pinning it to the world, I liked to think. But if you left the realm of the comic, where so much of punk actually lives (the huge and unacknowledged majority of it, from the Ramones to Green Day), or left the realm of self-directed maudlin anger (from Dinosaur Jr. to Nirvana, its own line), it felt very strange to be preparing violence in the way that was described. In Minor Threat, there was a plausible, *righteous* violence with which I still couldn't really identify—an interesting combination. Unfortunately, I didn't like the music all that much. It seemed rudimentary. And the righteousness wasn't mine, either. I wanted a better kind of musical fear and musical violence, one that would implicate me to the right degree and in the right way—and alienate me, too, in the right way. Luckily Becky K. was ready for me. She had another tape at hand.

Minor Threat didn't last long as a band. It was, though, as the music writers say, "influential." Meanwhile, its young singer, Ian MacKaye, moved through several short-lived bands until he formed another stable group, which added a second, lesser known but highly emotional young singer, Guy Picciotto, from the even shorter-lived (but "influential") band Rites of Spring. This was, as it turned out, a piling together of two geniuses on the Lennon/McCartney model—with a new rhythm section of comparable genius. They called their band Fugazi.

It chagrins me to be writing about Fugazi, since no one is less qualified than I am to do it. I wasn't there in D.C. when they started, I didn't see them on their first tour or their second, and I always had the profound and pleasurable sense that their music at least partly excluded me, because it was so tightly bound up with the post-hardcore and straight-edge world, a subculture I had nothing to do with. They were not commercial, they didn't offer themselves to the world through radio or TV, they didn't connect to anything else I knew or that felt natural to me. In fact, in addition to being a band, Fugazi was a kind of phenomenon known to many people who didn't care for them musically: an anticommercial, ultramoral, somewhat puritanical outfit that toured constantly, often playing in such unconventional places as church basements and college rec halls; that insisted on all-ages admissions to shows so that fans under eighteen or twenty-one could attend; that held down ticket charges as low as five dollars, rather than raking in the money. It was the apex of do-it-yourself. The band also maintained absurdly affordable prices on their recordings, which came out on MacKaye's own label, Dischord Records. (Dischord still survives, having released 157 albums and singles, mostly from other bands, over twenty-eight years of existence. They recently sent me a fresh cassette of the first Fugazi album for just four bucks, replacing the one I had dubbed without paying in 1989.)

I wanted a music whose formal violence would lead to something other than the demand for rioting, beating, or killing. I wanted . . . what? With Fugazi's first EP, here it was, this thing I wanted inchoately, on a seven-song tape, without time enough to breathe between songs. It was repeated on two sides of the same cassette so you could just flip it without rewinding and experience the explosive sequence again. *Fugazi* is a record I haven't been able to get out of my head for more than half a lifetime.

Return to that initial question: how does rock music produce the feeling of physical violence, especially if you subtract the lyrics for a minute before adding them back in? I'm afraid my answer is stupidly literal. I actually think it depends on rock being loud enough to cause aural pain, which it generally refrains from doing; and depends upon the instruments truly beating down on something, though not other human bodies.

The blues had the violence of threats, verbal promises of what was *going* to happen, echoed in the percussive guitar. But the promised violence also seemed limited in reach to the resonation of that wooden guitar, like the length of an arm or the extension of a shouting voice: it felt mano a mano. The bluesman might promise to cut you, and the ringing steel strings had the sound of cold metal. He could also promise to be Samson-like amidst Philistines; "If I had my way / I'd tear this building down," Blind Willie Johnson famously sang. But then the music itself couldn't produce that displacement of air, that concussion, of a wrecking ball that would put the building down. The speed-up of an acoustic guitar strum and the clang of the strings can always certainly be scary, or chill-inducing—in protest songs, too (take Dylan's "The Lonesome Death of Hattie Carroll"), which redress violence with righteousness—but nothing emulates a force that can really do damage, in a big way.

You need something properly loud to get more fear-inspiring effects. You need a bagpipe, a full symphony orchestra, or, in our time, major amplification. For the real violence of which rock is capable, you need an extreme degree of guitar volume and, I think, maybe above all, an amplified, highly articulated form of drum-kit drumming, learned from hard bop and everything that came after it, from such black jazz drummers as Max Roach and Art Blakey and Elvin Jones; a sound that then partially entered rock through such white players as Ginger Baker of Cream and Keith Moon of the Who and Mitch Mitchell of the Jimi Hendrix Experience. A drummer in a rock band can actually hit objects with remarkable facility—can strike physically, can beat on skin—and this striking or beating, rather than falling into straight rhythm, can in its most effective instances hold onto a movement of the unexpected, as when a tom hit or a snare roll or a cymbal crash drops in at any moment, and makes you feel it first as a kind of percussion upon or in your own body, and then as your own arm or foot punching down, to strike. A fully-amplified, distorted, and fed-back guitar, rather than leading at all times, can follow such drumming as part of the musical fabric, emulate it and respond to it, lock into it—thud along with the bass drum at one moment, and scream tunelessly as a drumstick strikes a cymbal at another. Then you have a new kind of artistry, a terrifying rock 'n' roll art of symbolized physical violence fully manifested.

The most interesting pop music is that in which the lyrics understand the moods made available by the instrumental parts, and then have a complex control over the encouragement of these moods, or a deliberate separation from them. The significance of Fugazi for me in 1989 was that they used an extreme, controlled musical violence to develop an ethos of separation—a combination of violent music and lyrics that opposed various forms of numbness and abuse that came violently, to everyone, from the outside: consumerism, sexual objectification, the obsession with sickness and health, and the use of drugs, legal and illegal, to drown it all. The music felt like a protective, preemptive assault, a use of musical violence, swinging outward, when the world would secretly do violence to you, pushing inward. Their sound was a bat skillfully wielded against projectiles; a cudgel to smash a kind of glassy or icy envelopment. Or, recognizing that the abuse had already inevitably made it inside you, the band tried to make you puke it out.

Only years later did I hear on live recordings the proof of what I'd heard about in school-talk at the time: Ian MacKaye sir-ing and ma'am-ing his audience, polite to a fault, deliberately friendly ("Good evening, everybody. How are you this evening?"; "What the heck"), before launching into another song of devastation. The conscious gentleness seemed to confirm the possibility of a music that could put the channeled eruption of violent emotions to work, not to wear out civilization, but to make a differently civilized, more careful, and radically reformed society.

Am I wrong to hear *Fugazi* as a story of development? That's how I've always interpreted it. "Waiting Room" starts with the well-known bass figure; then an off-time drumstick click; then the chugging guitar; until the song stops dead, proving total control. It restarts with a tattoo of drums. "I am a patient boy / I wait, I wait, I wait, I wait." The song really *is* about a waiting room. The singer is a patient—in the doctor's office sense—as well as someone forbearing to act. He watches everyone and everything else moving around him, but despite the movement, "they can't get up." The waiting room is like Plato's myth of the cave, everyone watching the images on the wall, moving their feet along, apparently living an exciting life, secretly in chains. Only MacKaye promises he's getting out, with youthful certainty: he's going to fight "for what I want to be." "And I won't make the same mistakes," he declares. To which Picciotto, singing backup, lisps, "Yes, I know"—in what has always sounded to me like a duplicitously, satanically soothing voice. Won't he make the same mistakes?

On "Bulldog Front," Picciotto tries out his own song of self-certainty. He's addressing a bad "you," an ignorant individual, someone who accepts everything as it is and defends his own turf. "Ahistorical . . ." he sings. "My analysis: it's time to harvest the crust from your eyes."

Picciotto again on "Give Me the Cure." He delivers an absolutely direct lyric, as if his own eyes have now cleared, and he's discovered something worse than he'd ever imagined. "I never thought too hard on dying before." Face to face with the fear of sickness, he sings of the ways society promises it could fix it, should fix it— and can't or won't fix it. These are the lyrics that always get to me:

> *But you've got to—*
> *Give me the shot*
> *Give me the pill*
> *Give me the cure*
> *Now what you've done to my world?*

Ian comes back in, and shouts the lyrics along with him, as the bass, guitar, and drums reach their most concerted attack, ending on a drum roll and the entire combo stopping short as Guy screams: "Give me the shot!"

I took the album literally, as being about a society in which you're fixed; even your actions, even your violent actions, are fixed; and wherever you would get up, or speak, you are forced to watch; and the ultimate model of it all is medicine. Behind the album, for me, lurked the doctor's office (and his waiting room), and the medicine a doctor could give, and how little this would help. I also knew when I was listening to the album that I was so far alienated from the culture from which the music was speaking, that, probably, I was completely wrong interpretively—this was only how *I* felt. I presumed they were thinking of drugs, intoxicants, hard living—things I didn't know. Lacking a context to bind me, I figured it *could* be about medicine, about a medicalized society, about the fear of death managed and organized to make us beg constantly for help that won't come. That's certainly what scared me, where my fears lay.

Where MacKaye went in another song, "Suggestion," was pure late-'80s cultural politics. The protagonist wants to know why he can't walk down the street free of sexual suggestion. He is singing, it becomes clear, as a woman. She ought to be free of male harassment, objectification, of an entirely false vision of "what it is to be a man." It's a use of the bellowing violence of hardcore to argue for restraint and politeness and righteousness: a paradox. At the end, MacKaye steps out of this weird ventriloquism into the cool third person, seeing the man's sense of entitlement, the woman's being herself and only herself, and how, because the rest of us keep quiet and won't speak up, this all ends in evil, maybe rape. "We keep quiet like they taught us . . . / We blame her for being there / But we're all here / And we're all—GUILTY!" Exactly the words Becky K. had spoken to me to explain Minor Threat.

• • •

I finally saw them in 1991, at the Channel, a now-defunct rock club along the Fort Point Channel in Boston. I stood back from the stage about forty feet, to the side of the second of two mosh pits that had developed. Nightclub-type tables had been moved aside and grouped around the piers that held up the ceiling, which gave the shaved-headed, shirtless male dancers extra platforms from which to dive into the crowd, when they weren't confronting each other in a battering-ram whirl, soaked white T-shirts swinging from their belts. I've read how unpleasant it could be for the band to play in front of jerks at rock clubs, once they grew too big to play the church halls. They did it so they could be heard by their new larger audience of suburban lunks like me, for which I'm still grateful.

And yet, in front of this crowd, as opposed to on my headphones, the whole point of the music seemed lost. The sense of exclusion was in the music, somehow, but by letting us all in to hear their message the message was wiped away. I remember the band as bored or annoyed. They were as great as they should have been, but with this crowd they seemed to know there could be no transcendence. They barely spoke, and eventually gave up most of their pleas to get people to be nicer to each other, to be mindful of the mixed boys and girls at the front of the stage singing along, to stop shoving into them—they had made these pleas often enough, to enough crowds. And yet it didn't seem to work now.

There was no blood on the floor, there were just people constantly colliding in the pit, and lone young men like stags lifting their knees in a fright-dance, heads down, waiting for someone else to charge them. I remember the scene, I remember a couple of songs, but the one truly dramatic moment I *think* I remember is when Fugazi stopped playing, and there was no change or loss of intensity in the violent moshing. "You don't really care what we do?" asked Ian from the stage. "You don't care if we play or not?" And at that moment— when, in the lore of Fugazi, it would seem the crowd should have come to its senses, become ashamed, settled down—it seemed true, that those moshing teens really didn't care. The musical violence just seemed to allow a game of simulated violence on the dance floor. It seemed to me that maybe Fugazi really wouldn't play anymore; it seemed like the thing they *should* do, just pack it up and leave, if this was what they were in the presence of. But, presumably for the benefit of everyone who'd paid and stood listening, they played the rest of their set, and got their applause at the end.

So *this*, I thought, leaving, crestfallen, *is still what the world is like.* I was scared again, not from the music, but from the kids I had seen, and the sense that even in the presence of the "best" kind of musical violence, purgative, restorative, political, instructional, guilty, my little ideas or hopes didn't always work.

For some reason—bullheadedness, or stupidity— I've held to an idea since, and always believed there is pop music that must do *something*. Specifically, it should reform people's ideas, or at least remind them of what they already ought to know; preserve for them a certain mood, or thought, or hope, which they need to have. It ought not just to be a joke, to say that there are albums that can change your life. But this may have been the ultimate fantasy, from the get-go; and if I had accepted the unreliability of pop, its falsity, at fourteen, maybe there would have been less heartache since.

# 5
## TINY BIG DREAMS

Talking Heads: *Remain in Light* (Sire Records, 1980)
### John Haskell

I was a poet, but I didn't know it. Or maybe I did. When I was a kid I had to walk through a kind of canyon to get to my school, and although it wasn't far, it was far enough so that walking along I used to memorize poetry. I didn't think of it as actual poetry, but like poetry, the words spoke of longing and isolation, emotions I was vaguely aware of, and also of love, an emotion I could only imagine. The words invoked a world that was beyond my world, but by saying them over and over I was putting them into my brain and making them mine. And I spoke them out loud because they were songs. They were songs my mother brought into our house. She was the one who normally bought the records, and although she wasn't musical, and didn't even seem that interested in music, because of her I listened to Harry Belafonte and Joan Baez, to Rodgers and Hammerstein and Frankie Laine. And also Simon and Garfunkel. At that time there was a record called *The Sounds of Silence*, or maybe that was the title of a particular song. "Hello darkness, my old friend." I remember the lyrics printed on the album cover, referring to Emily Dickinson and Robert Frost and to a poem by E. A. Robinson about a man who ought to be happy but ends up killing himself. I was lucky to have Simon and Garfunkel, and especially Simon, who wrote the words, because for the most part Simon and Garfunkel didn't sing love songs. I'd never been in love and I didn't understand love, but I understood these songs. Using a miniature cassette tape recorder I would record these songs off our family's high-fidelity phonograph and then go into my room, into my bed, and under the covers I would listen, not to the music but the words, rewinding and replaying the words that were describing the human condition. Which even then I recognized as *my* condition. Because I was remembering the words, and sometimes falsely remembering them, and possibly *because* I was falsely remembering them, one day, walking home through the canyon, it occurred to me that I could add to the description of that human condition. It was a thought in the form of desire. And so I started writing. I didn't call it poetry at the time because my desire was to write something else. I sat at a piece of furniture in my room, a so-called secretary with a fold-down tabletop, and I wrote what were essentially notes to my nascent self. They were lyrics, and one of them, which I can still remember, was about "having big dreams, but thinking of you." When they were finished I would read them to my sister, and she was always encouraging, but I wasn't writing them for her. I was writing them, not even for me. It was just the pleasure of attempting to corral my imagination. In searching my young heart for the words to describe melancholy and hope I was discovering melancholy and hope, and also joy. And there was a kind of thrill in the discovery of a mode of thinking and feeling that resonated, both with who I was and who I imagined I would be.

I rented a room in a farmhouse in the Santa Cruz Mountains. The room had one bed, one chair, and I sat in the chair, looking at the pasture out my window, writing poetry. I was also reading poetry, going to the university library and checking out books, usually by the Beats, and one day, following some trail of thought, I stumbled into a listening booth. I remember the black console, and wearing very large headphones, and listening to Ezra Pound recite his *Cantos*. He'd adopted a strange version of an Irish accent, and whether it was the words, or the way he said the words, I heard in them a musicality. I was enrolled at the university, and one of the classes I took was a dance class, taught by someone named Tandy Beal, and because I was taking her class, and enjoying it, I went to dance performances at the university. Most of them were pretty bad, but one night I remember seeing a performance set to Steve Reich's "It's Gonna Rain." What I remember is the one dancer, alone on stage, and a man's voice on the loudspeakers saying, "It's gonna rain," over and over. And that was the music. It was a song by Reich, or maybe composition is a better word, or maybe decomposition, because the phrase was repeated over and over until, over time, the words overlapped and blended together, and it wasn't clear exactly what they were doing, or saying, and it didn't matter. By shedding their old meaning they'd taken on both a meaning of their own and a life of their own, and they seemed to be living that life. It was a glimpse, I thought, into a world in which words were capable of transcending themselves, and I liked it.

I was living in New York, trying to become a writer, living in a variety of rented rooms. One of them was on the Bowery, in a long open apartment on the fifth floor, and one day, while I was walking through Soho, I saw a notice, taped to a door, for a dance class. Normally I wouldn't have paid attention, but this particular class was taught by Lucinda Childs, well known at the time for choreographing *Einstein on the Beach*. Although I didn't know her work, I knew her artistic lineage, and I knew it was a lineage I wanted to find out more about. So I signed up. In the beginning there was a lot of stretching and limbering, but mainly the class was about making dances. I didn't know what the other students, in their black leotards, were doing.

They obviously had a more traditional training than I did, and in fact I wasn't a dancer at all, I was a writer. Lucinda seemed to be aware of this, and when I told her what I decided to make for the class she was encouraging. It was a dance in which words—the words I was writing—would be the music to my so-called choreography. I wanted to integrate the words and the music and also the dance, and by joining content and form create not a *gesamtkunstwerk*—although I liked that word—but a language that would, by moving beyond language, describe the world. And because I would dance the dance I would have to *be* the world. And when I presented my piece during the final week of class Lucinda seemed to like what I was doing, or at least the direction in which I was going, and it seemed to me like a direction in which I could go even further. But when I sat at my writing desk by the large window, trying to write the words, trying to find the exultation and sorrow that would animate the dance, the only words I could muster were the same old prosaic words I was trying to transcend.

My writing career, such as it was, had become entwined with my so-called performance career; the only public exposure my writing had was when I performed it, usually at small, obscure, temporary venues in lower Manhattan. I was writing every day, trying to make my writing a little more like life, trying, in a musical way, to express that life. And of course it wasn't easy. Music was music, and words were something else, and although I recognized the difference, I wanted to bridge that difference. With words. And because I knew someone who knew someone, I was given a chance to perform at a club on the Lower East Side called Darinka. It was more a dance club than a performance space, but on certain nights they opened the stage for performances, and it was open on the night I performed there. I invited a few people and a few other people were there, and they were standing on the dance floor and I was standing on the stage, and then I started performing. I started telling a story I'd written and then memorized, and the story was meant to communicate, in a musical way, something about life. But because it wasn't music, because I was asking words to perform a function that wasn't their function, the story didn't work. Or maybe the performance didn't work. Either way, I could see that the people in the audience didn't understand what I was trying to do. At first they listened, but then they started talking, and then a few of them started heckling, and the more they didn't understand, the more I wanted to convince them. Of life, or the spirit of life, or something there was, but after a while I hardly knew what it was, or what it was I was even saying. In retrospect, I'm sure I was utterly incomprehensible, but I kept saying things, altering my story bit by bit until finally I jettisoned the story and started to improvise, changing it into a description of what I was feeling, which was more and more about the necessity of communicating. I was speaking, following the impulse of my improvisation, making less and less sense and at the same time feeling more and more frustration at my words and their inability to break through the barrier, or at least my barrier, and the words, these words, these things that were meant to mean something, became just meaningless, just nonsense, even to me, and certainly to everyone else. During what would have been the middle of the performance, acting the part of a demented performance artist, I jumped off the stage, dodged past the remaining spectators, and ran out the door.

I was living in Chicago, in a storefront apartment with Mary Lou, and when Mary Lou would leave for work, if I was home, I'd use our "dining room" table as a writing desk. I would sit there for hours, reasonably sure I had something to say but without the desire to say it. And so I didn't get much done. Mary Lou would come home and she'd jokingly ask our pet canary what I'd accomplished that day. If I'd written anything I'd read her the words I'd written, and she would listen, thoughtfully, and she was encouraging, but because the words didn't mean anything to me, they meant even less to her. The canary, whose name was Pee Wee, sometimes sang while I was reading. His singing seemed random to us because we couldn't hear the world he heard, but there were definite moments when he was inspired, and by inspired I mean literally, as if some breath was compelled to come out of him. Considering the size of his tiny body, his singing was huge, and we'd listen to him, trying to decipher the message he was sending, and then, after a while, the singing would stop. One day Mary Lou left for work and I was sitting there at my makeshift desk, trying to remember the impulse that got me to sit at a desk in the first place. And since I wasn't actually writing, to distract myself I put on some music. I put on a tape of *Remain in Light* by Talking Heads, and I noticed, at a certain point during a certain song, Pee Wee started singing. It seemed as if maybe his singing was triggered by a particular song, a song about "these hands . . . passing in between us . . ." and as an experiment I rewound the song and played it again, and at the same point in the same song he started singing again—it was an instrumental part—and his singing reminded me of joy. I was very aware of joy because the joy I'd once remembered feeling had long since disappeared. So I just sat there, listening to the melodies of the song interweaving, and the words of the song were interweaving, and there was Pee Wee, interweaving with the whole thing. This is like life, I thought, like things happening at the same moment, or at the same mental moment, and to hear these various melodies, or even some of them, I had to relax my brain, and as I listened, at some point my brain did finally relax, because that's when Pee Wee's melody, happy and joyful and loud, became clear. He was singing *with* the music, and he was singing *for* the music, singing the thing he had to sing, clear and strong, and there was no mistaking joy, I could hear it, the joy and the desire, and the joy *of* desire. It was coming from deep inside his tiny breast or brain, and it wasn't about the words because he wasn't using words, and *because* he wasn't using words, I think I understood what he was saying.

# O BLACK AND UNKNOWN  BARDS

*American Primitive Vol. II: Pre-War Revenants (1897–1939)*
(Revenant Records, 2005)

## John Jeremiah Sullivan

The Americans have only a few Negro songs.
—Josef Goebbels, *Diaries*, May 3, 1942

Late in 1998 or early in '99—during the winter that straddled the two—I spent a night on and off the telephone with a person called John Fahey. I was a junior editor at the *Oxford American* magazine, which at that time had its offices in Oxford, Mississippi; Fahey, then almost sixty and living in Room 5 of a welfare motel outside Portland, Oregon, was himself, whatever that was: a channeler of some kind, certainly; a "pioneer" (as he once described his great hero, Charley Patton) "in the externalization through music of weird, even ghastly emotional states." He composed instrumental guitar collages that were assembled from snatches of other, older songs. At their finest they could become harmonic chambers in which different dead styles spoke to one another. My father had told me stories of seeing him in Memphis in the summer of '69, when he introduced his "Blind Joe Death" routine at the fabled blues festival, appearing to inhabit, as he approached the stage in dark glasses, the bent form of an aged sharecropper, hobbling and needing to be led by the arm. Fahey meant it as a postmodern prank at the expense of the white, authenticity-obsessed country blues cognoscenti, and was at the time uniquely qualified to pull it. Five years before he'd helped lead one of the little bands of enthusiasts, a special-ops branch of the folk revival, who staged barnstorming road trips through the South, trying to find surviving notables from the pre-war country blues or "folk blues" recording period, 1925 to 1939.

What is country blues? We don't exactly know. We can however define the enigma very clearly by tracing the career of a single song. Crying Sam Collins's "Yellow Dog Blues," made in 1927, is an ethereal piece performed on slide guitar, one of the masterworks. It includes the lyric, "I'm goin' where the Southern cross the Yellow Dog." (That was railroad slang for Moorhead, Mississippi, where two lines, the Southern and the Yazoo Delta—Y.D., Yaller Dawg—came together.) The song calls to mind something W. C. Handy, the legendary black Memphis composer, claimed to have heard a quarter century earlier on a train station platform in Tutwiler, Mississippi, where he nodded off and woke to the "plunking" of a "lean, loose-jointed Negro." That was in 1903. The man fretted his guitar like a Hawaiian, with a slide, in this case the back of a knife blade. "'Goin' where the Southern cross the Dog,'" remembered Handy. "The singer repeated the line three times, accompanying himself on the guitar with the weirdest music I had ever heard."

There's the appearance of an unambiguous correspondence between the man on the platform and the man on the record (at least one blues writer has implied they could be the same person), which would make the country blues a pre-recording form, a folk form, miraculously taken unawares and amberized on fragile shellac discs. But in fact there's an invisible musicological vastness between the two songs, which are connected not by an arrow but by a labyrinth. W. C. Handy couldn't forget that melody, nor the line about "the Southern." In 1914, after a passage of more than ten years, they wove their way into his "Yellow Dog Rag," published as a sheet-music number. Another decade went by, the song was an orchestra standard, an early jazz band recording, a medicine show tune. In 1924 it became a blues-queen hit after Bessie Smith did it backed by New Orleans guys. This is at the advent of so-called race recording, meaning, simply, music marketed to blacks. "Yellow Dog Blues" sold thousands of copies, North and South.

Crying Sam Collins heard it. His lyrics show a clear familiarity with the Bessie Smith version. Or rather, one that's suggestively unclear. A lot of their poetic effect comes from Collins's obvious misremembering and reshaping of a phonograph he caught somewhere, maybe through a window. This so often happened in the blues. As the lyrics got twisted, they got more interesting. As a piece of entendre, "Easy, rider, don't you fade away" is pretty bald when a woman sings it, whereas the openness of Collins's "Be easy, mama, don't you fade away"—what does that mean? Is she going to fall asleep while he makes love to her? It's some other kind of fading away he has in mind.

There you have the problem of the country blues: is it folk, or is it commercial? Folk that has somehow gone out, wrapped back around, and re-inserted itself into its own tradition through the tentacle of the new recording medium? No old-time American form arrives burdened with more Authenticity than the country blues, but is it actually *originary* in any way? Is it pop? Is it possible to have a commercial pop form that is identical with but still somehow ersatz in relation to an earlier pre-recording folk form? In Senegal I once met a maker of wooden masks who showed the group I was with a coffee-table Picasso book that inspired his designs. It had pictures of broad-planed abstract faces that Picasso had learned from the man's ancestors. Is the country blues a sped-up version of that?

John Fahey spent an unwholesome portion of his life gnawing these and similar questions. He'd grown up well-to-do in Washington, D.C., obsessive from an early age about old guitar playing, fingerpicking. After college he went west, to a grad program in ethnomusicology, then at a deciding moment dropped out, essentially to hunt old bluesmen. He took part personally in the tracking down and dragging back before the public glare of both Booker T. Washington "Bukka" White and, in a crowning moment, Nehemiah Curtis "Skip" James, the dark prince of the country blues, a thin black man with pale eyes and an alien falsetto who in 1931 recorded a batch of songs so sad and unsettling it's said they paid him on street corners not to sing them. Fahey and two associates found James in a charity hospital in Tunica, Mississippi, in 1964, dying with cruel slowness of stomach cancer. *We know you're a genius,* they told him. *People are ready now. Play for us.*

"I don't know," he is said to have answered. "Skippy tired."

I'd been instructed to get hold of Fahey on a fact-checking matter. The magazine was running a piece about Geeshie Wiley (or Geechie—and in either case likely only a nickname or stage moniker, meaning that she had Gullah blood, or that her skin and hair were red-tinted). She's perhaps the one contemporary of James's who ever fully equaled him in the scary-beauty department, his spiritual bride. All we know about Wiley is what we don't know about her: where she was born, or when; what she looked like, where she lived, where she's buried. She had a playing partner named Elvie Thomas, about whom even less is known. (Elvie has no rumors even.) Musicians who claimed to have seen Geeshie Wiley in Jackson, Mississippi, offered sketchy details to researchers over the years: that she could have been from Natchez, Mississippi (and was maybe part Indian), that she sang with a medicine show. In a sadistic tease on the part of fate ("History practicing its scissor-clips / In the dark," wrote Charles

Simic), the Mississippi blues scholar and champion record collector Gayle Dean Wardlow—he who found
Robert Johnson's death certificate—interviewed, in
the late '60s, a white man named H. C. Speir, a onetime
music-store owner from Jackson who'd moonlighted
as a talent scout for several pre-war race labels. Though
Speir almost certainly met Wiley around 1930 and told
his contacts at the Paramount company in Grafton,
Wisconsin, about her—he may even have taken the
train trip north with her and Elvie, as he was known
to have done with other of his "finds"—and though at
least two of Wiley and Thomas's six surviving songs
(or "sides," in the favored jargon) had been rediscov-
ered by collectors when Wardlow made his '69 visit to
Speir's house, they were not yet accessible outside a
clique of two or three aficionados in the East. Wardlow didn't know to ask about her, though he was closer
at that moment than the people who were coming to
know her voice again, closer than anyone else would
ever get, sitting half a mile from where she'd sung,
talking with a man who'd seen her face, watched her
tune her guitar, put out her cigarettes.

Few ciphers have left behind as large and beguiling
a presence as Wiley. Three of the six songs she and Elvie
Thomas recorded are among the greatest country blues
performances engraved into shellac, and one of them,
"Last Kind Words Blues," is an essential work of American art, sans qualifiers, a blues that's not a blues, that's
something other, but is at the same time a perfect blues,
a pinnacle.

People have argued that the song represents a lone survival of an older, already vanishing minstrel style, others that it was a one-off spoor, an ephemeral hybrid that originated and died with Wiley and Thomas, their attempt to play some tune they'd heard somewhere, by a fire. The verses don't follow the A-A-B repeating pattern common to the blues, and the keening, loosely modal melody isn't like any other recorded example from the period. Likewise with the song's chords: it opens with a big plonking, menacing E but quickly withdraws into A minor and hovers there awhile, key-wise (the early blues was almost never minor). The serpentine dual-guitar interplay is no less startling, with little sliding lead parts, presumably Thomas's, moving in and out of counterpoint. At times it sounds like four moving hands obeying a single mind and conjures scenes of the endless practicing that becomes more of a compulsion after a while, a thing in the midst of which other things are periodic interventions, and of how well the two women knew each other, the discipline of their musicianship, the vast boredoms of the medicine-show world. The words begin:

*The last kind words I heard my daddy say,*
*Lord, the last kind words*
*I heard my daddy say,*

*"If I die, if I die, in the German War,*
*I want you to send my money,*
*Send it to my mother-in-law.*

> *"Well, 'f I get killed, if I get killed,*
> *Please don't bury my soul.*
> *I cry, Just leave me out, let the buzzards eat me*
>    *whole."*

The subsequent verse had a couple of unintelligible words in it, whether from mumbling on Wiley's part or because of the heavily crackling static that comes with the territory where old, invariably deteriorated 78-rpm discs are involved. One could hear her saying pretty clearly, "When you see me coming, look 'cross the rich man's field," after which it sounded like she might be saying, "If I don't bring you flowers, / I'll bring you [a boutonniere?]." This verged on nonsense—more to the point it was non-idiomatic. But the writer of the magazine piece wanted to quote the line, and my task was to work it out, or at least prove to the satisfaction of my bosses that this couldn't be done. Ed Komara, in those days the keeper of the sacred B.B. King Blues Archive at Ole Miss, suggested contacting Fahey. Actually what I think he said was, "Only John Fahey knows stuff like that."

After a lot of my phoning around, an old front-desk attendant gruffly agreed to put a call through to Fahey's room. From subsequent reading I gather that at this time he was making the weekly rent by scavenging and reselling rare classical music LPs, for which he must have developed an extraordinary eye, the profit margins being almost imperceptible. I pictured him prone on the bed, gray-bearded and possibly naked, his overabundant corpus spread out like something that only got up to eat: that's how interviewers would find him, in the little profiles I'd read. He was pretty well hampered at this point by years of addiction and the bad heart that would kill him two years later, but he'd been famously cranky even before all that, so I was taken aback to find him ramblingly familiar from the moment he picked up the phone. A friend of his to whom I later described this conversation said, "Of course he was nice—you didn't want to talk about *him*." Fahey asked to have fifteen minutes to get his "beatbox" hooked up and locate the tape with the song on it. I called him back at the appointed time.

"Man," he said, "I can't tell *what* she's saying there. It's definitely not 'boutonniere.'"

"No guesses?"

"Nah."

We switched to another mystery word, a couple of verses on: Wiley sings, "My mother told me, just before she died, / 'Lord, [precious?] daughter, don't you be so wild.'"

"Shit, I don't have any fucking idea," Fahey said. "It doesn't really matter, anyway. They always just said any old shit."

That seemed like the end of our experiment. Then Fahey said, "Give me about an hour. I'm going to spend some time with it."

I took the tape the magazine had given me and went to my car. Outside it was bleak north Mississippi cold, with the wind all but unchecked by the slight undulations of flatness they call hills down there; it formed little pockets of frozen air in your clothes that zapped you if you shifted your weight. I turned the bass all the way down on the car's EQ and the treble all the way up, trying to isolate the frequency of Wiley's vocal, and drove around town for the better part of an hour, going the speed limit. The problem words hesitated to show themselves, but as the tape played over, the song itself emerged around them, in spite of them, and I heard it for the first time.

"Last Kind Words Blues" is about a ghost-lover. When Wiley says "kind"—as in, "The last kind words I heard my daddy say"—she doesn't mean it like we do; she doesn't mean *nice*; she means the word in its older sense of *natural* (with the implication that everything her "daddy" says afterward is unnatural, is preternatural). Southern idiom has retained that usage independently in phrases involving the word "kindly," as in "I thank you kindly," which—the *OED* bears this out—represent a clinging vestige of the primary, archaic meaning: not *I thank you politely and sweetly* but *I thank you in a way that is meet, or natural, given your deed*. There's nothing "kind," in the everyday way, about the cold instructions her man gives for the disposal of his remains. That's what I mean about the blues hewing to idiom. It rarely makes mistakes like that.

He's died, as he seems to have expected—the first three verses establish that, in tone if not in utterance. Now the song moves into a no-man's-land: she's lost. Her mother warned her about men, remember, "just before she died." The daughter didn't listen—they never do—and now it's too late. She wanders.

> *I went to the depot, I looked up at the sun,*
> *Cried, "Some train don't come,*
> *Gon' be some walking done."*

Where does she have to get to so bad she can't wait for the next train? There's a hint, since she's still talking to him, or he to her, one isn't sure. "When you see me coming, look 'cross the rich man's field"; if I don't bring you *something*, I'll bring you *something else*, at least that much about the lyric was clear—and part of an old story: if I don't bring you silver, I'll bring you gold, etc.

Only then, in the song's third and last movement, did it get truly strange:

> *The Mississippi River, you know it's deep and wide,*
> *I can stand right here,*
> *See my baby from the other side.*

This is one of the countless stock or "floating" verses in the country blues—players passed them around like gossip, and much of the art to the music's poetry consisted in arrangement rather than invention, in an almost haiku-like approach by which drama and even narrative could be generated through sheer purity of image and intensity of juxtaposition. But what's Wiley done with these lines? Normally they run, "I can see my baby [or my "brownie"] / From this other side." But there's something spooky happening to the spatial relationships. If I'm standing *right here,* how am I seeing you *from the other side*? Unless I'm slipping out of my body, of course. Going to join you *on* the other side. Wiley closes off the song as if to confirm these suspicions:

> *What you do to me, baby, it never gets out of me.*
> *I mean I'll see ya,*
> *After I cross the deep blue sea.*

It's one of the oldest metaphors for death and was ready to hand in 1930, thanks to Wiley's non-secular pre-war peers. "Precious Jesus, gently guide me," goes a 1926 gospel chorus, "o'er that ocean dark and wide." *Done gone over.* That meant dead. Not up, over.

Greil Marcus, the writer of the piece I was fact-checking, noted the extraordinary "tenderness" of the "What you do to me, baby" line. It can't be denied. There's a tremendous weariness too. "It never gets out of me"—yeah, and part of her wishes it would, this long disease, your memory. ("The blues is a low-down achin' heart disease," sang Robert Johnson, echoing Kokomo Arnold echoing Clara Smith echoing a 1913 sheet-music number written by an Italian American and titled "Nigger Blues.") There's nothing to look forward to but the reunion death will bring. That's the narrow, haunted cosmos of the song, which one hears almost as a kind of reverberation, and which keeps people up at night. We know the sentiment, even the three-part structure—*you're dead but won't get gone; I'm lost; I'm coming to join you, baby*—from traditional Irish songs like "I Am Stretched on Your Grave."

One was having an intense time of it in the old Toyota. But when I got back onto the phone with Fahey, he was almost giddy. He'd scored one: *blessèd*. That was what her mother told her, "Lord, blessèd daughter, don't you be so wild." I cued up to that line. He was right. It seemed self-evident now, impossible to miss. I complimented his ear. Fahey cough-talked his way through a rant about how "they didn't care about the words" and "were all illiterate anyway."

That nervous swerving between ecstatic appreciation and a reflex to minimize the aesthetic significance of the country blues was, I came later to see, a pattern in Fahey's career—the Blind Joe Death bit had been part of it. It's possible he feared giving in too far to the almost demonic force this music has exerted over many— or worried he'd done so already. I'm fairly certain his irony meter lay at zero when he titled his 2000 book of short stories *How Bluegrass Music Destroyed My Life*. More than that, though, the ability to flick at will into a dismissive mode was a way to maintain a sense of expert status, of standing apart. You'll find the same tendency in most of the other major blues wonks: when the music was all but unknown, they hailed it as great, invincible American art; when people (like the Rolling Stones) caught on and started blabbering about it, they rushed to remind *everyone* it was just a bunch of dance music for drunken field hands. Fahey had reached the point where he could occupy both extremes within the same sentence.

He'd gotten about as far as I had with "[a boutonniere?]," which technically remained the matter at hand, so we adjourned again. Came back, broke off. This went on for a couple of hours and grew increasingly hopeless-seeming. I couldn't believe he was being so patient, really. Then at one point, back on the road, after more rewindings, some tiny fibers at the edge of my innermost ear bones detected a faint "l" near the beginning of that last word: b-o-L-t? Bolter? A scan through the OED led to "bolt," then to "bolted," and at last to this 1398 citation from John de Trevisa's English translation of Bartholomeus Anglicus's ca. 1240 Latin encyclopedia, *De proprietatibus rerum* (*On the Order of Things*): "The floure of the mele, whan it is bultid and departed from the bran."

Wiley wasn't saying "flowers"; she was saying "flour." The rich man's flour, which she loves you enough to steal for you. If she can't get it, she'll get bolted, or very finely sifted, meal.

> *When you see me coming, look 'cross the rich man's field.*
> *If I don't bring you flour,*
> *I'll bring you bolted meal.*

Fahey was skeptical. "I never heard of that shit," he said. But later, after we'd hung up for what seemed like the last time, he called back with a changed mind. He'd rung up other people in the interim. (It would be fun to know whom—you'd be tracing a very weird and special little neural pathway in the fin-de-siècle American mind.) One of his sources told him it was a Civil War thing: when they ran out of flour, they started using bolted cornmeal. "Hey," he said, "maybe we'll credit you in the liner notes if we ever get this new thing together."

Fahey never saw the new thing. It remained in the planning stages when he died. On the phone he talked about Revenant, the self-described "raw musics" label he'd cofounded in 1996 with a Nashville attorney named Dean Blackwood. Revenant releases are like Konstruktivist design projects in their attention to graphic detail. One could go to school on their liner notes. Now Fahey and Blackwood were planning a new release, which would be all about pre-war "phantoms" like Wiley and Thomas (and feature new, superior transfers of the pair's six sides). The collection's sole delimiting criterion would be that nothing must be known biographically regarding any of the artists involved, and every recording must be phenomenal in a sense almost strict: something that happened once in front of a microphone and can never be duplicated, only experienced. Fahey and Blackwood had been dreaming this project for years, refining lists. It was curation as art. And I'd contributed a little ant's mouthful of knowledge. Fahey said goodbye for real and left me to enter my suggestions on the fact-checking sheet.

Almost six years passed, during which Fahey died in the hospital from complications following multiple-bypass surgery. I assumed with other people that he'd taken the phantoms project with him, but in October 2005, with zero fanfare and after rumors of Revenant's having closed shop, it materialized, two discs and a total of fifty songs with the subtitle *Pre-War Revenants (1897–1939)*.

All persons interested in American culture ought to find a way to hear this record. It's one of the most important archival releases since the Robert Johnson box that alerted my generation to the existence of the pre-war blues, maybe even since Harry Smith's seminal *Anthology of American Folk Music* in 1951, and for the same reason: it's less a scholarly effort to preserve and disseminate obscure recordings, indispensable as those undertakings are, than the charting of a profoundly informed aesthetic sensibility, which for all its complication and occasional torment was passionately, selflessly in communion with these recordings and the minutest nuances of their artistry for many decades. Fahey had dissolved into this music. At one point late in his life a rich aunt died and left him a bundle of money. He put it all into Revenant and went on living at the welfare motel. He was just being consistent. You have to remember that when Fahey went looking for Skip James in the first place, he was motivated partly by a desire to rehabilitate James's stature, sure, but more largely by the desire to learn from James certain unorthodox fingerings and tunings without knowledge of which the maestro's songs were impossible to duplicate. Fahey knew he couldn't honorably strip them and tear new compositions out of them until he'd learned to play them shading for shading. James's minor-key tunings—the reason his music seems to sob out of the grooves on its opening notes—were supposedly taught him by a mentor who'd learned them from Bahamian soldiers during World War I (the old West Indian world that the South grew out of, a world of mingling slaves). Wherever those chords came from, Fahey watched the old man's hands and unlocked them. This was apprenticeship of the soul. On *Pre-War Revenants* you're in a room with that soul's owner, himself now a postmodern primitive revenant, and he's playing you his favorite records. That's the scenario Fahey wanted to enshrine.

Doing it right involved remastering everything fresh from 78s, which in turn meant summoning a transnational rabbit's warren of the so-called serious collectors, a community widespread but dysfunctionally tight-knit, as, by process of consolidation, the major collections have come into the keeping of fewer and fewer hands over the years. "The serious blues people are less than ten," one who contributed to *Pre-War Revenants* told me. "Country, seven. Jazz, maybe fifteen. Most are to one degree or another sociopathic." Mainly what they do is nurse decades-old grudges. A complicated bunch of people, but for reasons perhaps not entirely scrutable even to themselves, they have protected this music from time and indifference. And the collectors were first of all the finders. Those trips to locate old blues guys started out as trips to canvass records. Gayle Dean Wardlow became a pest-control man at one

z

z

point, in order to have a legitimate excuse to be walking around in black neighborhoods beating on doors. "Need your house sprayed?" Nah. "Got any weird old records in the attic?"

It was the shellac—that's why they got so rare, these 78s. Shellac was a crappy material. They used it for the race records. During World War II it was suddenly in great demand; there was an artillery gun that used it, I think. The old records inevitably got scrapped. Most of them. Of course the other thing that happened is all sorts of people went into the attic to box up and retrieve their old 78s, which flushed the stuff out into the swap-meet world. Something like 60 percent of the songs on *Pre-War Revenants* are SCOs, Single Copy Only.

The names alone are a poem. Most often they're all that's left to put beside the sounds. Blues Birdhead, Isaiah Nettles, Bayless Rose, Pigmeat Terry, singers that only the farthest gone of the old-music freaks will have heard. "I got the mean bolita blues," sings the unknown Kid Brown. ("Bolita" was a poorly understood Mexican game of chance that swept the South like a hayfire about a hundred years ago and wiped out a bunch of shoe box fortunes.) These songs are flashbulbs going off in immense darknesses. In the 1920s and early '30s a great musical harvest happened in the South. John Fahey was, after Alan Lomax, one of the first people to point out how much better a job the Northern race record labels did at recording the phenomenal *breadth* of pre-war black Southern styles than did the much-romanticized university-trained "songcatchers," who tended to have ideas about what was legit and what was crude. The labels, having for the most part no real access to or interest in the opinions of Southern blacks about music or anything else, but recognizing a market there, compensated by recording everybody, then reprinting and rerecording those artists who by whatever mystifying calculus of taste sold more copies than others. Any two girls who walked in, anybody whose cousin said he was the best singer in two counties, drunk, stoned. Come on in. What is that, rubber bands on that thing? Sit right there. Kazoo jazz? Slap it, boys. There's kazoo jazz on *Pre-War Revenants*. You laugh but it'll singe your topknot it's so electric.

The first song is Homer Quincy Smith's "I Want Jesus to Talk With Me," recorded in the winter of 1926. Here's what's known of Homer Quincy Smith: a man by that name once entered into a makeshift recording room with a giant harmonium around his neck, an instrument he made sound as though he'd ripped it from the chancel of a medieval cathedral and swum with it to the New World, all the while refusing to curse God. It is not hard to feel something of Fahey's pleasure at the thought of people careening into mailboxes when this song is the first thing to emerge. Blackwood's liner notes are gonzo kicks throughout. On this song he's merely accurate:

> *A moon shot that lands somewhere out in the great yearning beyond, leaving the era's mannered quartet spirituals in the dust. Who the heck*

*was the audience for this record? Does Smith
know? Does he care? Hardly. He and his cata-
comb organ have gone celestial-plane on you. . . .*

Blackwood goes on to suggest that the reason
Smith didn't appear in the discography again until '29
is that it took him the three years to recover from these
recordings.

It provokes nervous laughter after a while, how
many musically worldview-demolishing songs there are
on this collection. There's a guy named Tommy Settlers
who sings out of his throat in some way. I can't describe
it. He may have been a freak-show act. His "Big Bed
Bug" is about all there is of whatever he was. There are
also some classic, ragged blues, songs like the Mississippi Moaner's "It's Cold in China Blues" ("So cold in
China, birds can't hardly sing") and Henry Spaulding's
"Cairo Blues" (pronounced Karo), both of which speak
to the staggering range of melodic variation that singers
were able to get out of good old I-IV-V, A-A-B, after
generations of tunneling out those forms. Academically
I'd known that was true from having listened to Harry
Smith's *Anthology* and heard songs like Richard "Rabbit" Brown's "James Alley Blues," one of the wildest,
loveliest, most fiercely wavering songs: "Sometimes I
think that you're too sweet to die . . ." To hear many
more comparable examples for the first time is astound-
ing. In 1935 a singer named Otto Virgial did a song
called "Little Girl in Rome." That is, Rome, Mississippi;
or maybe Rome, Georgia. In either case, he got a letter

from her this morning saying "she got something for" him and is "gonna bring it back home." Otto Virgial played the guitar as if it might save him:

*Yon' come my baby,*
*Coming down the line,*
*With her headlight*
*Just shining light,*
*That pushes all behind.*

In what is surely a trustworthy mark of obscurantist cred, one of the sides on *Pre-War Revenants* was discovered at a flea market in Nashville by the person who engineered the collection, Chris King, the guy who actually signs for delivery of the reinforced wooden boxes, put together with drywall screws and capable of withstanding an auto collision, in which most 78s arrive for projects like these. The collectors trust King; he's a major collector himself (owner, as it happens, of the second-best of three known copies of "Last Kind Words Blues") and an acknowledged savant when it comes to excavating and reconstructing sonic information from the wrecked grooves of pre-war disc recordings. I interviewed him a couple of years ago. A perk of magazine journalism is you can call up fascinating strangers and ask them questions on absolutely no pretext. King, like Fahey, graduated with degrees in religion and philosophy. He described "junking" that rare 78 in Tennessee, the Two Poor Boys' "Old Hen Cackle," which lay atop a stack of 45s on a table in the open sun. It was brown. In the heat it had warped, he said, "into the shape of a soup bowl." At the bottom of the bowl he could read the word *perfect*: that's a short-lived hillbilly label. "Brown Perfects" are precious. He took it home and placed it outside between two panes of clear glass—collector's wisdom, handed down—and allowed the heat of the sun and the slight pressure of the glass's gravity slowly to press it flat again, to where he could play it. Now he could begin finding out what it remembered.

King said at this stage in the process he visualizes the battered grooves of the record as being "like a swimming pool, in the way it dips down from three feet to four feet to five, and the deep end is the bottom of the groove." As he talked I watched a twelve-year-old in a diving mask groping the pebbly bottom of some huge public pool, looking for an all-but-invisible thing he wasn't supposed to have lost, his retainer. King has no way of knowing where the "signal"—the magnetically engraved molecular imprint of the soundwaves—is strongest, or is even present. "Somewhere in there," King said, "as you move up the slope—it could be at the very top, it could be anywhere in between—there's some residual signal you can tap into." He said he routinely goes through twenty or thirty different styli trying to isolate that signal. On days off he'll hit junk shops and buy old phonographs to experiment with them on junk records, picking up new tools in the needles. A straight, narrow needle drops to the bottom of the groove; the fatter it gets, the farther up the walls you're feeling as you pass by. These are differences of microns.

Sometimes, King said, he can tell things about the record's life from how the sound has worn away. The copy of Geeshie Wiley's "Eagles on a Half" (there's only one copy) that King worked with for *Pre-War Revenants* had, he realized, been "dug out" by an improvised stylus of some kind—"they used anything, sewing needles"—in such a manner that one could tell the phonograph it spun on, or else the floor underneath the phonograph, was tilted forward and to the right. Suddenly you have a room, dancing, boards with a lot of give, people laughing. That's a nasty, sexy song: "I said, 'Squat low, papa, let your mama see. / I wanna see that old business keeps on worrying me.'" King tilted his turntable back and to the left. He encountered undestroyed signal and got a newly vibrant mastering of that song. Indeed listening to it in juxtaposition with earlier attempts is color after black-and-white.

Strangest of the songs, a recording for which something in me had to be restrained from trying to extract an explanation from King, is the very oldest, "Poor Mourner," by the duo Cousins & DeMoss, who may or may not have been Sam Cousin [sic] and Ed DeMoss, semi-famous late-nineteenth-century minstrel singers—if so, then the former is the only artist included on *Pre-War Revenants* of whom an image has survived: a grainy photograph of his strong, square face appeared in the *Indianapolis Freeman* in 1889. These two performed "Poor Mourner" for the Berliner company in 1897. Berliner patented disc as opposed to cylinder recording—easier to duplicate. (The mourner's bench was where you went to sit when you had a guilty conscience.)

The first two bars of this song are possibly the freakiest thing I have ever heard that was also on some level pop music. Dual banjos burst forth with a frenetic rag figure, and it seems you're on familiar if excitable ground. But somewhere between the third and fourth measure of the first bar, the second banjo pulls up, as if with a halt leg, and begins putting forward a modal dronish thing on top of the first instrument, which twangs away for a second or two as if it hadn't gotten the memo about the imminent mood change. Then both banjos grind down together, the key swerves minor, and without your being able to pinpoint what happened or when, you find yourself in a totally different, darker sphere. The effect is the sonic equivalent of film getting jammed in an old projector, the stuck frame melting, colors bleeding. It all takes place in precisely five seconds. It's unaccountable. Chris King said, "That is not a function of some weird thing I couldn't fix." I asked if maybe the old machines ran slightly faster at the start. He reminded me that the song didn't start with music, it started with a high voice shouting, "As sung by Cousins and DeMoss!" The music doesn't start till three seconds in.

Most of the lyrics are unintelligible to a degree that makes Geeshie sound like an elocution tape, but a couple of verses can be decrypted with help from historical sources. One particular couplet pops up in various spirituals and period ditties and reflects—depending which scholars you trust—either an old Protestant injunction against crossing one's feet when walking (since to do so is to dance) or, more innocently, a scrap of "fiddle-sing," telling the dancers what to do:

*Now, mind now, sister, how you step on the cross,*
*Your foot might slip and your soul be lost.*

When this song comes on I invariably see my great-grandmother Elizabeth Baynham, born in that same year, 1897. I touched that year. There is no degree of remove between me and it. I barely remember her as a blind, legless figure in a wheelchair and afghan who waited for us in the hallway outside her room. Knowing that this song was part of the fabric of the world she came into lets me know I understand nothing about that period, that very very end of the nineteenth century. We live in such constant closeness with the abyss of past time, which the moment is endlessly sucked into. Viktor Shklovsky said, "Habit devours objects, clothes, furniture, one's wife, and the fear of war. Art exists to restore the sensation of life . . . to make the stone stony." These recordings let us feel something of the timeyness of time, its sudden irrevocability.

# BEAUTIFUL NOISE

Kate Bush: *The Sensual World* (Columbia Records, 1989)
## Stacey D'Erasmo

In 1989, toward the end of the last century, Kate Bush's *The Sensual World* was released, and I didn't think much of it. I played it, I kept it around, but it seemed excessive. Velvety. Weird. I didn't know anything about art then, certainly nothing about music (still don't, really); maybe a little bit about writing, but not much. My emotions and the emotions of my friends and lovers were what seemed most critical, as if the world might tilt differently on its axis from the weight of what we felt, or didn't feel; said, or didn't say. It was like our art, collectively. Which is embarrassing.

But true. Around then, those of us in our late twenties weren't very ironic. Desperation, urgency, and smoking were virtues. Remember: things were bad. We think they're bad now, but then we were only a few years into

AIDS, Reaganomics and Thatcher still ruled the world, and the talk at our all-day, drunken brunches often concerned whether or not they were going to round up all the gay people and put them in camps. (This seems less paranoid when you remember that there were actually serious proposals being made to quarantine the HIV-positive.) It seemed as if something playful and feathery and kissable—our adolescence, in the '70s—was being ground into dust. People were already beginning to drift away; some of them died. My friend Kent looked terrified and I kept thinking that he was going to stop looking terrified soon, that he'd move into acceptance, that the panic rising off him in waves would ebb into poetry. It didn't. Afterward, his parents took all his paintings and locked them in their garage in Connecticut. Kent's lover, an older man with a beard, was already dead by then. We all moved to Brooklyn, where nobody lived and the grocery stores were big and sad and rundown. We listened to Madonna and the Communards and the Pretenders. We quilled our hair into stiff spikes and spent our paychecks on leather jackets. We felt like survivors. We knew about the trains, which car to ride in, and how; on dark streets, you carried your keys poking between your fingers, weaponlike. We stayed out late in places where punky strippers danced on the bar.

So I thought Kate Bush's sixth record was naive. She made so many strange noises: beeping, hooting, ringing, sighing, screeching, impersonating, invoking, murmuring like someone rolling over in bed. Maybe we had once thought that life would be like that, that the future was filled with fearless young women spread out along the horizon line, foraging, thoughtful, but now we knew better. She seemed, and perhaps was, dancery, fanciful, dreamy, innocent, self-important. On the cover of *The Sensual World*, her shoulders are bare and her mouth is covered by an enormous flower that seems to be a camellia; the points and curves of Bush's face are no less flowerlike. The music was so beautiful, and reveled so in its own beauty. She seemed husked, recklessly sensitive, and all too aware of being sensitive, like a girl in her room, making things up late at night in front of the mirror.

Young, we would have called it, my friend Norah and I, in one or another of our cruddy kitchens. *She's really young,* we might say of an acquaintance, a friend, a girlfriend, probably one another, secretly. It wasn't a compliment. We thought a lot of people, perhaps most people, were young, and we felt sorry for them. Kate Bush seemed young to me. In fact, she was about our age; in fact, though I didn't tell Norah this, I had known about Kate Bush before I got this record because I knew Pat Benatar's cover of her 1978 hit "Wuthering Heights." I was in love when I first heard that version of "Wuthering Heights," lying in the back of a car one summer afternoon, still in the scrubs I had to wear to the abortion clinic where I worked with great earnestness and great boredom, hurtling over the Brooklyn Bridge for reasons I now can't remember. I just remember the cables of the bridge, and the sound of someone who loved someone else so much she didn't even know she was dead. Tapping at the windowpane, begging. *Let me in. I'm so cold.* I fell out of love a few months later, and I didn't think about "Wuthering Heights" for many years.

If I say that I had to be in love again to take *The Sensual World* to heart, to play it over and over until it became one of those records that has the status of an imago for me, one of my most private selves, it will sound as if I mean that it's a great record about romantic love, or sensuality, or that it reminds me of someone with whom I used to listen to it at twilight, or whatever. None of that is the case. It's more wiggly than that, at an odder angle. When I fell in love again, I felt that I had arrived in a different country, a smaller and more tender one. Things that I had disdained suddenly seemed vital. In a second, I was done with spikes, done with Brooklyn, done with Norah, done with doom. Because I was in love, I got it: the vast web of a life, every string vibrating.

*The Sensual World* is unapologetically womanly, a fresco of relatedness: lover to lover, mother to child, child to father, woman to self, woman to computer, woman to book (how many pop songs have referenced Joyce's *Ulysses*?), woman to anything that can be coaxed into making a noise. There are more sounds on *The Sensual World* than I can name; Bush's voice is itself a most peculiar instrument, much too high and pinched, and yet so uncannily gorgeous. I had to be in love to understand *The Sensual World* initially, because it's easiest in that state to be so ferociously yielding. In love, I was willing to be that weird, that awkward, that uncritical and omnivorous. It was a record when I first had it, big as a kite; later, a CD; now, it lives among the shades on my iPod. But I remember it best as a tape, with a splotch of some sort of fruit juice on the hard plastic case, the corner of the case smashed, the case usually empty, tossed onto the floor of the car as we drove out of the city.

All these years later, it's the abundance of *The Sensual World* that still knocks me flat. It begins with the distant sound of bells on the title cut; the bells segue into a murmur, a *yes* that then winds into a sinuous reimagining of Molly Bloom's soliloquy as a pop aria that sounds like a lament; farther in, you find the delicate suspended notes of "This Woman's Work"; the tenderness toward everything that breathes, or even doesn't, as in her ode to her computer, "Deeper Understanding"; farther still, the sighs, the voices, the hauntedness, the yearning, the strange wheezings, the sounds of pipes, something that sounds like a chorus of Munchkins, someone singing in Bulgarian, the mad embrace of it, both figuratively and sonically. "Stepping out, off the page into the sensual world" was the line I loved best, and for a long time I thought I knew what that meant: escaping the dry, black marks, the fence of abstraction, for the wildly unpredictable richness of the world. Indeed, there is a kind of argument, or poetics, in *The Sensual World* concerning worldliness—that worldliness isn't only how much of the world you've seen or know, but how much of the world you can sense. How much of it has had its way with you and transformed you.

The '90s were also the years when I became a writer, and I began to understand that kind of worldliness as an *ars poetica*. That excessive hunger and curiosity. The willingness to wade into the material world and attempt to imitate all its sounds: the chirping, the ringing, its farts (which Bush leaves out, actually), its secrets, its shouts. If a woman felt a great affinity with her computer, what would that be like? Bush had no qualms about imagining it. The particularity of the interior landscape that Bush describes, the idiosyncratic connections and resonances, the texture, were part of what I was trying to teach myself how to do in that decade through the long hours at my own computer. *The Sensual World* literally references a novel, Joyce's *Ulysses*, but it's also as if it somehow intuits the kind of dense emotional substrate that forms the core of a novel. On that record, form follows feeling rather than the other way around. You want—I want—a novel to be like that, to be that unguarded, that wayward, that distinctive. Love may have been the spur, but it led me into a very different way of looking at things. I began to understand the value of being almost ridiculously impressionable. I wrote a book, then another.

Of course, I had misunderstood her.

The abundance is certainly there, but how did I manage to overlook all the sadness on that album, the deep melancholy of it? Even her earlier composition "Wuthering Heights" is terrifying, proto-goth. There is always, in Bush's songs, a chilling wind blowing through the beauty. In the video for "Wuthering Heights," Bush makes herself disappear. The camera trick is silly; her outfit is worse; but the idea still cuts: she's dead, hopelessly lost. She can't come back. I had edited that part out somehow, carried away by the intensity. I, too, had wanted to feel that much—too much, more than I could stand. I wanted to go much too far. Now, listening to *The Sensual World*, I can't believe what I didn't hear all those times that I popped the cassette into the deck in the car all those summer and winters: the ghosts. It's a haunted album. The mood is decidedly retrospective, if not elegiac. That camellia: it's not ornamental, it's an emblem of the transitory. We cram it in, but we can't hold it. The world passes. The people we love are on the other side; they can't hear us. I did become a writer, which I thought could never happen, but the rest of that life dissolved.

You're left with the lines you remember: a few lyrics ("like a Machiavellian girl"—what is that?), the field with the horse in it that you always saw as you rounded the corner towards home. The memory of the small click as the tape ended, then the comment, "I don't like that record. She's spooky."

The tape is gone, and the car is gone, and the house belongs to someone else, and the field with the horse in it is probably still there, but I'm not. I kept the battered tape, a few other things. I've noticed since that the particular timbre of a voice is the last thing to fade, that you still hear it long after the person has left the room.

# MENTAL CHICKENS

*Topless Women Talk About Their Lives* Soundtrack
(Flying Nun Records, 1997)

## Todd Pruzan

**W**hy on earth was I reading about Winston Peters? Who was Winston Peters to me? This gadfly I'd never heard of, this radical-centrist Maori activist politician hustling for issues I'd never encountered, half a world away? And I mean that literally, by the way: there are 8,153 miles of land and ocean between my old apartment on Roscoe Street in Chicago and Peters's home district of Tauranga, on the Bay of Plenty in northern New Zealand. A nation so discreet that mid-1990s reports of a brewing race war, replete with terrorist threats and car attacks and fears that a spark could ignite a full-on antipodean Belfast, barely surfaced in the Northern Hemisphere. But I'd seen an article, somewhere, and the unlikeliness of it all made Winston Peters a great talking point, I thought, if I should happen to encounter a Kiwi at a party.

At this particular party, in December 1997, there were two. Scott and Nomi, both redheads with rare accents of jumbled vowels, stood on the wood-frame back landing, pausing to catch their breath in mid-retreat from a couple of years in high-finance London—and, it emerged, a couple of years as a couple. They were on a long layover, visiting friends before returning to Auckland, and they were amiable enough, chatting together over their plastic cups. Wouldn't they be floored that some dude in Chicago, in dumb, thick America, could be interested in the ins and outs of their homeland? I had my card—I played it: "So, um, hey. What's this Winston Peters guy all about?"

I understood my mistake instantly. Both faces scrunched, both heads reared backward. Scott sighed, then nodded: "Ahhh . . . *Winston Peters.*" Obligingly, he offered a brief Petersology, but clearly he wasn't so much impressed as unsettled. Lesson learned: coming to a party armed with quiz-night insignifica doesn't mean you should necessarily lock and load. If I'd been the one interloping at an Auckland house party—*Hey, that alderman of yours in Chicago, Bobby Rush: bit of a bomb-thrower, is he?*—I might have inadvertently sprayed my host with a mouthful of Steinlager.

At least I wasn't wearing my Chills T-shirt. Because no sooner had I stopped asking after New Zealand's legislators than I became a full-on pest, ticking off a laundry list of the bands I'd caught at Lounge Ax, the humid indie-rock club lit entirely by Christmas lights that stood just across Lincoln Avenue from the alley where John Dillinger had been shot to death. The Chills. The Bats. Bailter Space. The Jean-Paul Sartre Experience. Straitjacket Fits had left the biggest impression of all, midway through a cardiologically punishing triple-bill (dubbed, aptly, the Noisyland Tour); their albums were full of ethereal shoegazer swirls, but live, they'd played the loudest, heaviest gig of my life, and my last without earplugs—

*Hey, so where'd Scott go? Must've run into someone. . . .* Nomi seemed charmed, though. Maybe she was homesick. New Zealand didn't have much of a reputation in this self-absorbed city. Chicago's sense of itself, at least to its troops of privileged, aggressively unassuming postgrads, had shifted from acting like New York's resentful sibling to adopting a pose of defiant independence. It had rock music down, that's for sure. Nirvana's ambush from Seattle on America's record stores and radio formats had fully consumed itself by then, but the attack had fed precious oxygen to Chicago's holy trinity—Smashing Pumpkins, Liz Phair, and Urge Overkill, three brief candles keeping a hopeful, cynical city in their sway. And Lounge Ax was the tiny high temple, a joint where guitar heroes cheered on other guitar heroes. In 1995, a new neighbor to the club had filed a noise complaint, accidentally setting into motion the bar's eventual demise, but the silver lining was *The Lounge Ax Defense and Relocation Compact Disc*, an unparalleled mid-'90s time capsule capturing the roaring Jesus Lizard, the rageful Shellac, the curiously geometric Tortoise, the drunkenly defeatist Mekons, and even such sympathetic blue-chip contributors as Sebadoh, Superchunk, and Yo La Tengo.

*¡Olé, Chicago!* It was almost enough to make me want to stick around. But not quite. I'd already joined the enemy; I was leaving for New York a month later. New year, new city, new world. A wholly predictable pilgrimage—and, from Chicago, a predictably traitorous one. But I wasn't alone. Nomi, it turned out, would be moving to Manhattan in a month as well.

So we traded e-mail addresses. She was a year or two older than me and wore a default expression of wry amusement. And she was a music fan, albeit a less annoying one. "That *Lounge Ax* album sounds great," she said. "And you know, you're reminding me, there's this movie that just came out in New Zealand . . . you'd like the soundtrack."

Nomi and I made landfall days apart, eager, shell-shocked. Over dinner we traded CDs, and the joke that wasn't really a joke: that we were, empirically, the Two Most Freaked-Out People in New York. She was already laughing at her new city—her hotel room at the W, impossibly pretentious yet barely larger than its own bed, and her subway commute to Grand Central, with a mob of employees sprinting for the crosstown shuttle like a siege of cranes. She was like a New Yorker from another country, already devising ways to keep her head together: "I just have to remind myself to do all these sorts of mental chickens."

*Hmm—must be a Kiwi thing. "On your bike!"* ("Fuck off!") *"A box of birds!"* ("It's all good!") *"Mental chickens!"* Months earlier, working as a reporter, I'd sat in a Chicago bar one morning with a bunch of expats to watch them watch live soccer via satellite, and an Ulster bricklayer had recounted his favorite World Cup matches for me: "Scotland vairsus Spain, Norway vairsus Addeleigh." It had taken me hours to unspool "Addeleigh" as the boot-shaped Mediterranean peninsula where they make formaggio and chianti and Ferraris. "Mental chickens" took some teasing out, too. But even after I'd slapped my forehead the next day—mental *check-ins!*—I'd agreed with Nomi. Truly, there's no finer condition for the care and breeding of mental chickens than the first month of an open-ended New York City residency. And I can't imagine a truer document of my mental chickens than the CD Nomi had brought me from Auckland, the soundtrack to a Gen X drama called *Topless Women Talk About Their Lives.*

The album seemed like the perfect complement to the Lounge Ax CD I'd handed her. And even before I listened to *Topless Women*, I saw that it looked like something she'd borrowed from my CD collection rather than something she'd added to it. Slivered artfully at the top and bottom of the cover are two horizontal shots of the cast, a Maori and four pale-faced *pakeha* (as some white Kiwis call themselves), lounging on a living-room futon. The title gets top billing, though, set at deafening point size in deadpan Helvetica Extra Bold. (Well, c'mon—it's a hell of a title.)

Not to disappoint, but let's be clear: *Topless Women* is not about pole-dancers. Yet I don't associate the title with the movie, either; I associate it with queasiness, sleeplessness, and rattled nerves. Ten years after moving to New York, my life seems impossibly removed from the one I had when I arrived. It's a paradox of time's fun-house-mirror elasticity that a year can seem trivially quick, a mere sprint to the crosstown shuttle—yet ten strung together are momentous, epic. There's no way to tally the great rewards and petty infuriations of belonging in the morass of New York, of knowing a setting that can make anyone feel so accomplished and buoyant and burned.

Never mind that it wasn't conceived to accompany a New York life: *Topless Women* was a curious soundtrack for my first year. I was twenty-seven when I installed myself on the parlor floor of a brownstone in Brooklyn, renting beautiful dark-brown hardwood floors and an airy fourteen-foot ceiling from a grim, unsmiling landlord from Wichita who could've been the model for Grant Wood's farmer in *American Gothic*. In his fussy museum of a living room, five doors south of Fort Greene Park, I signed documents in triplicate and tried to brace myself for those moments I knew were on their way, when I'd be staring at the ceiling with my heart racing because it was six o'clock in the morning and I didn't know where to buy a carton of orange juice and I was suddenly, absolutely alone.

There was a time in the late 1980s and early 1990s when music critics seemed immersed in a real New Zealand moment, cheering on the ascent of an artistically (though not commercially) influential label called Flying Nun, whose artists carved out a national genre and supplied the spark to a pop movement in America. Its indigenous sound isn't so instantly familiar as a Maori tattoo. But the laid-back garage-y guitar and aimless vocals were charmingly indifferent both to precise notes and global market forces, as though news of Duran Duran and Madonna hadn't yet undulated across the Pacific to New Zealand's rusty docks.

Or maybe being a punk rocker on a remote island nation, bobbing out there in the middle of the ocean, was like singing in the shower, where you could just belt it out, loud, loose, guessing vaguely at the melody, and sometimes even hitting it, but it didn't matter, because nobody was listening. (The Chills, a Flying Nun band from the South Island university town of Dunedin, actually had deaf fans, students who thronged the band's earsplitting gigs, moshing along to the floorboard vibrations.) But then again, New Zealand has long seemed the unheard, invisible Canada to the dominating United States of Australia. A few years ago in a Sydney music store, I asked a clerk to tell me about a CD I'd found, a compilation released by Dunedin's Arc Café. He turned the disc over indifferently, then shrugged and handed it back. "Dunno, mate."

Early punk on Flying Nun seemed attuned to vintage sounds from Liverpool and L.A., a timeless chime with amicable, jittery organ, rather than the era's more familiar rage and revolution. New York was awash in attitude, London in anarchy—and New Zealand?

Something more like ambivalence. This was surf punk, all right, but with no sunshine, no Dick Dale twang, just gunmetal skies and wet suits, menacing waves and hopeless search parties. It's the same ambivalence you could hear a decade later in the American indie rock it inspired: brooding, lackadaiscal music by Pavement and Luna and Superchunk.

Two Dunedin bands anchored the genre. David Kilgour's group the Clean churned like ocean undertow on urgent anthems like "Fish" and "Point That Thing Somewhere Else." And while the Chills could be cheerful—their signature song was a heavenly pop hit that was actually titled "Heavenly Pop Hit"— leader Martin Phillipps often used shimmering colors to conceal his darkest thoughts. A 1984 single, "Pink Frost," starts pink and quickly gets frosty, abandoning a breezy major-key intro for a hushed, uncertain four-bar phrase that ultimately dissolves into a spooked panic. "Wanna stop crying," Phillipps sings. "She's lying there dying / How can I live when you see what I've done?" Mental chickens.

The Clean and the Chills both take pride of place on *Topless Women Talk About Their Lives*. Like the most salient, inescapable soundtracks of the 1990s—Quentin Tarantino's *Pulp Fiction*, or Danny Boyle's *Trainspotting*—the album documents the personal vision of its director, Harry Sinclair. I was unfamiliar both with Brooklyn and with much of the soundtrack, and *Topless Women* pinpoints a jumpy mood.

Press play, and the soundtrack lurches into fifth gear

without warning. The 3Ds' "Hey Seuss," an opening-credits wail, unleashes guitars like sirens and distraught bullhorn vocals from a desperate singer who yelps like a drowning man. The Bats' "North by North" earns the Hitchcockian foreboding of its title, and Superette's gothic "Saskatchewan" oozes with icy, sexy cynicism. Straitjacket Fits's delicately latticed songs on *Topless Women* offset the Chills' jaunty "I Love My Leather Jacket," a sauntering tune that quickly yields to a characteristic gloom:

> *It's the only concrete link with an absent friend*
> *It's a symbol I can wear 'til we meet again*
> *Or it's a weight around my neck while the owner's free*
> *Both protector and reminder of mortality*

The weight around my neck doesn't lift until *Topless Women*'s closing track, Chris Knox's love song "Not Given Lightly," a cheerful, half-assed blues that swells over five minutes from acoustic strums into tuneful distortion. His serenade finally gets the grim soundtrack to crack a smile, almost a moment too late, but just in time for a happy ending.

We hit it off. But not like that. Maybe someone somewhere was pulling strings, holding me at arm's length: *You'll meet your wife in a few years—be patient. And being with Nomi—your heart would break. Oh, brother, in your life, you've never felt pain like that.* So we had tea. And drinks, and burgers and hipster parties in Greenwich

Village and Hell's Kitchen. There was a glint in her eye, even helpless laughter, when she told me about her absurd dating life, about the cardiologist from Weehawken who'd driven up in a Maserati and brought her to a pharmaceutical luncheon. And it took me some time to see beyond her humor. One evening, we sat at a bar at Spring and Elizabeth—Jeff Buckley's *Grace* was playing—and she somehow started talking about the night a few years earlier when she'd been raped on a kibbutz by a young guy, a family friend she'd trusted, who'd blamed her afterward for what he'd done to her. Maybe she'd only just remembered it. Maybe she'd just had to put it somewhere, and why not with her American younger brother?

In the fall of 2000, there was an e-mail to her friends. She'd been diagnosed. It was in her right breast. It was . . . not benign. Her vision had been deserting her, and she'd had fainting spells, and now she knew why. She was on leave, getting radiation. And even today I can't believe how she kept laughing. Well, why not? Because she'd also fallen in love: another Kiwi, a banker named Ian. They shacked up in a Spring Street loft, and he comforted her through her treatments.

I stopped over once at their place in 2002, to take in an orange June twilight from their balcony. She looked happy and exhausted. She'd been chosen as the face of breast cancer survival for a New Zealand ad campaign, and somehow that seemed like some kind of guarantee. And she and Ian were getting married, too. They were leaving for Auckland. Enough of New York. Time to go back home.

On my way out of their apartment, I rubbed the top of her head—for good luck? Her crew cut was recovering its way back to health. "At least yours is going to grow back," I said. She laughed. "You know, *every guy* says the same thing to me . . ."

The next January, from Auckland, she sent an e-mail to friends about how her summer was going—her new marriage; her return to intensive care; her now-complete blindness; her adorable new black lab puppy, Bleecker, photographed in a lush green garden. And six weeks later, in March, I got another e-mail. Subject: Nomi. For a few hours, I didn't even open it.

Ten years ago, I took a photograph of things that don't exist. August 1998, near the end of an afternoon amble across the Brooklyn Bridge. Nomi is in the foreground, shading her eyes and grinning serenely through a searing yellow haze. The World Trade Center looms behind her: two silent blue sentinels over lower Manhattan. I haven't seen the picture in years, and it seems impossible to believe that such a recent photo could be so full of ghosts.

Three years and one month later, my friend Joyce was crossing the Brooklyn Bridge into Manhattan, listening to My Bloody Valentine's *Loveless* in her Discman, when the first plane hit. She hasn't listened to the album since. I'm not going to claim that *Topless Women* holds such significance for me. In the weeks after September 11, I swaddled myself in Jamaican ska from the '60s, a hundred songs that comforted me like a wise elder: *the world is an old, old place, and it's going to keep on spinning.* But that lo-fi Kingston pop still bears the faintest residue of portent, of fighter jets whispering like UFOs over New York.

So what, then, is *Topless Women Talk About Their Lives*? The world's best unknown pop, by its best unsung artists? Hardly. My favorite album? Not even close. But after ten years, I can finally nail down its place in my autobiography. It's the album that brings me closest to that opening bell on my first New York decade. Proust had his madeleines; I've got Stereolab's *Dots and Loops*, Lambchop's *Thriller*, the Apples in Stereo's *Tone Soul Evolution*, and this CD: the only concrete link with an absent friend. But how much grief is appropriate for someone who's been woven neatly into my social fabric, and nothing more? Not a girlfriend, not a best friend— just a big spirit, someone I wish I could've introduced to more people, to my wife, to my daughter?

Maybe it's inevitable that New Zealand would represent for me a vivid tumble of life and death, a cheerful tune spiked with morbid, mordant lyrics. When I was twenty-five and working at an advertising trade magazine, a Sydney correspondent e-mailed one morning to tell us he was headed to Auckland, where his eldest daughter had died in a car crash. When I phoned him at a relative's house a few days later, his sister went to fetch him from her backyard, and the dangling receiver flooded my ear with the reverberations of morning songs: a box of birds, rejoicing on the other side of the world.

• • •

Some people dread their own nightmares. I'm more leery of those awesome dreams when I wake up grinning, momentarily unaware that I'm not as rich as I was a moment earlier, that the hatchets aren't buried after all, that the absent friends are still absent. I used to think it was impossible that I might not remember what's happened the previous day, or week, or five years earlier. But here I am, wondering about a friend who's almost entirely vanished. There's no e-mail to reread anymore, nothing to find on Google, nothing but a compact disc. I occasionally wonder what she'd think of what my New York life has become, with my new family and my hemispheric shift from a decade earlier, when I had time to wonder about things that didn't matter, like local politics 8,153 miles away, and *Topless Women.*

I still marvel at the album's yin-yang of delight and unease. And maybe that's what the director intended—capturing, in homegrown pop music, the nervous urban generation in Auckland a decade ago. Not that I would know. I've never been to New Zealand. And I still haven't seen the movie.

# ELEGY FOR A DISCARDED ALBUM

Pearl Jam: *Ten* (Epic Records, 1991)

## Joshua Ferris

It may be impossible to separate an album from its extramusical interference. The cultural noise is too disruptive. Try to listen to *Pet Sounds* without hearing the phenomenon of surf rock or the bicker of Wilson family dysfunction. Put on *Let It Be* without standing amazed at how far the Beatles had come from the British Invasion or detecting their quickening disintegration.

Similarly it's hard for anyone who came of age in the 1990s to disentangle Pearl Jam's *Ten* from the cultural detritus of grunge. Kurt Cobain and Company broke into the mainstream first and made grunge a household word, though in retrospect Nirvana seems less grungy than a singular post-punk phenomenon based around the conflicted charisma of the blond waif with the yeti's howl. Nirvana ran wildly disparate genres through the punk filter to such distinctive effect that to circumscribe them with the grunge label seems too restrictive. Which leaves *Ten*-era Pearl Jam, nearly twenty years later, the more likely to connote what the word popularly indicated: a deglamorized presentation made up of plaid shirts and duct-taped Chuck Taylors, lyrics and attitudes of youthful, earnest angst, and a declared hostility to the corporate machine that would eventually and inevitably co-opt it.

The word "alternative" in rock-and-roll history has two meanings. The different meanings divide two eras. The first refers specifically to a type of music that came of age in the '80s and early '90s and that offered a genuine alternative to the mainstream, to the windblown buffoonery of hair bands and the vapid ubiquity of shrewdly marketed pop that had played on Chicago radio stations all during my high school years. (There was classic rock, too, Led Zeppelin and David Bowie and Pink Floyd, indisputably proven but codified and domesticated, recycled on radio as much to give earlier generations a chance to wax nostalgic as to introduce a new generation to its excellence.) Within a very short period of time, alternative music became so popular and sold so well that "alternative" suffered an Orwellian inversion: the alternative designation was soon just another frequency on the FM dial, and could not be used unironically by anyone who knew the word's first meaning.

Before they became "alternative," Pearl Jam was among the alternative—perhaps not as stark an alternative as Mudhoney or Sonic Youth or Mission of Burma or

Fugazi (*Ten* was released by Epic, after all, not Sub Pop or Dischord), but an alternative all the same. Especially to a kid living in the Chicago suburbs who worked in the mall soliciting passersby for consumer surveys. My employer was called Facts in Focus. The pay was good but arguably not worth the humiliation, the scorn, and the mineral avoidance of eye contact. A casual drive to the mall, a leisurely stroll to the Sunglass Hut, a mindless stop for a Cinnabon was radically recontextualized in light of my presence, clipboard in hand, asking for a moment of some shopper's time. Standing by the benches and fake plants, I endangered many unscripted agendas. No thank you, no time, not now, no way, get real, are you kidding kid, maybe on the way out. My only happiness was the cigarette I would smoke in the Arby's at the food court during my ten-minute. Mortification was seeing someone I went to school with walk by on her way to Abercrombie and Fitch. I owned all of Sting's solo work and my best friend was in a band that played covers of Queensrÿche and Tesla. I was several karmic rungs below the punk ethos.

But by senior year, I was sick of buying what Sam Goody told me to buy. I had started to detect the musical conservatism that ruled *Rolling Stone* magazine. I loved Pink Floyd, but my fixation had settled on the unheralded, difficult material—the psychedelic masterwork *The Piper at the Gates of Dawn*, the minimalist concept album *The Final Cut*. A cassette of R.E.M.'s *Reckoning* showed up in my car, I don't know from where, but I started choosing to play it over yet another spin of the

Eagles' *Greatest Hits*. A friend of mine at school, whose outsider status was reinforced by his penning a music zine called *Puke and Guts*, full of animated graphics of puke and guts and articles on metal and hardcore, turned me on to Faith No More's *Introduce Yourself*. Not exactly Minor Threat, but not "Fields of Gold," either. Another friend, an unrequited crush, played the Pixies' *Doolittle* for me in her car as we sat parked outside a forest preserve.

For most of high school I'd been the ignoramus. Spoon-fed received wisdom, the ignoramus is culturally illiterate. He is sheltered and predictable. He takes his cues from the broadest of sources. He wouldn't know a decent album if the jewel case came up and bit him on the ass.

But then the ignoramus hears things—in my case R.E.M., the Pixies, and some early punk—that sound unlike anything he's heard before. He's floored. The music hits him like a revelation. It changes his life. He gives no thought to those who would shake their heads with distaste at the weird new sound. He gets it. The discovery is major. His growing disgust with the status quo is finally explained. He can no longer be complacent with the mediocre. It doesn't matter how clangorous or marginal the sound is. In fact, the farther out of the mainstream, the more intensely attached he becomes. The ignoramus transitions into the initiate.

Suburban kids, unaware of cool things but suspecting they exist, are convinced of being the only living souls inhabiting a passed-over land whose zombie residents are reconciled, even satisfied, with their fate.

When the kids discover something that sounds like it comes from a place of refuge and nourishment, they grab on body and soul, which is what I did in the fall of 1991. I turned from ignoramus into initiate. I was finding the underground.

In reality the underground was finding me. Others, better informed, knew that many of the important developments in the indie music scene that made Nirvana and Pearl Jam and the entire grunge phenomenon possible had taken place the decade before. They knew that, by 1991, Seattle had grown sick of the "Seattle sound," and that A&R men had plundered it and packaged it with a nifty narrative and marketed that package to kids just like me. Those better informed might have considered *Ten* derivative of better albums by better bands, bands that had been relegated to small labels that sent their albums to independent music stores on consignment and a prayer. Bands that chose to forge a new sound on college radio instead of playing by the rulebook of payola popularity. Bands that had paid fealty to the indie ethos for years. They might have thought of *Ten* as a "corporate, alternative, and cock-rock fusion," in Kurt Cobain's words. But to me, *Ten* was a marvel. It was a relief from the half-baked crap then passing for music. Unlike vapid pop it was earnest, oblique, and hard-hitting. Unlike hair bands it was genuine and unadorned. And unlike classic rock it was happening now, it was of my time.

What I immediately loved about *Ten* was its purity of emotion and restless aggression. I was surprised by the discovery of such music and by my depth of feeling for it. Eddie Vedder's strong voice, pulling off the neat trick of always being fanged and clawed while also always vulnerable, was the band's big appeal. There was an overwhelming amount of emotion in that voice; it seemed to say, *To keep these songs inside of me would mean suicide.* He was full of accusation, disappointment, outrage, and sorrow, but I'd never encountered anything half so life-affirming.

I listened to that album endlessly. I did a lot of car listening, both driving and parked, and I listened to it locked away in my bedroom. I stayed home from parties to listen to it. I left people to be alone with it. It could make me bang my head, jump on the bed, and sing at the top of my lungs. It could also make me stare straight ahead like a damaged person, unblinkingly, with eyes glassy with tears—not tears of pathos or woe-is-me but the blown-mind kind, tears of transcendence.

*Ten* made me rapturous. It said, Here is another way of listening to the world. Here is another world entire. It annihilated the dreary sameness that characterized the suburbs: not even this place can be dull if it contains this music. Familiar streets in familiar subdivisions were no longer a chore to drive down, because I had *Ten* playing. Conducting surveys in the mall wasn't as odious, because I could run through the songs in my head and anticipate listening to the album when work was through. And I knew something, I possessed something vital that the benighted mall dwellers knew nothing of. It was as if I'd fallen in love. The same alchemy was involved, the same renewal and passion, the same giddy hope.

Could a single album really do so much? Some of my reaction might have had to do with timing. With a final semester of high school remaining, I already had one foot out the door and standing on the college campus. I was about to leave behind the confines of cliques and conformity and move toward freedom and discovery. *Ten* hinted at this wider world. It suggested the music I would soon discover: Fugazi, Guided by Voices, the Velvet Underground, *The Songs of Leonard Cohen*, PJ Harvey's *Dry*, Pavement, Liz Phair's startling first album.

But projection can't account for the immediate visceral joy that came from listening to *Ten*. Remember those intense, soul-bearing marathon conversations in high school with the person you believed you would love forever, the ones that went long past midnight, and that left you feeling like no one had ever connected as you just had with the one who understood you best? I had that feeling when I pressed play.

Part of the album's appeal, unfortunately, a small but not insignificant part, was bound up with my sense of having discovered it. It was my secret and mine alone, a short-lived illusion made possible by Nirvana.

Nirvana was fresh, loud, irreverent, challenging, catchy, and true. It was also widely exposed very quickly. Even my Deadhead friends were in thrall. They were just as happy to pull on their one-hitters to "Smells

Like Teen Spirit" as to "Ripple." For someone just getting up the nerve to shun the popular, I was reluctant to embrace *Nevermind* with the same fervor as the other suburbanites.

Plus Nirvana seemed to have a lock on the sound. There was only one Michael Jackson, only one Madonna. How much room did the public have for a band so distinctive, raw, threatening? *Nevermind*'s eclipse looked complete.

I did not love Nirvana nearly as much as I love them today for this simple (and stupid) reason: at the time, they received a too-swift and all-consuming collective embrace. No, I was making myself into the outrider, the musical pioneer. I liked this other band. It was every bit as anthemic and generationally relevant as *Nevermind*, but nobody was really paying attention to it.

The outrider is what the initiate becomes after he forgets his former life as an ignoramus. He dismisses anything smacking of the masses or widespread exposure, oftentimes without regard to the music itself. Chart-toppers are spurned. Discovery of an unknown act bestows upon the outrider a street cred that cannot be found in the magazine rack or in his older brother's vaults. New music must spring out of the underground for it to pass the litmus of acceptability. The outrider passes the new album along to one or two like-minded friends, but only if they can be trusted. That way the music remains a secret possessed only by vetted and qualified believers. If and when the time comes that the album, through the sloppy maintenance of word of mouth (or through "selling out" to a car commercial, or through an upgrade to a label with greater marketing chops), reaches a saturation level, a tipping point into mass media coverage and consumption, the outrider condemns the newcomers as arriving "late" to the album—the atomic bomb of indie insults—and forsakes the album. It's forsaken in a fit of pique: how dare a band I discovered be taken over by others? If the outrider loves the album enough, the forsaking, if entire, will feel a lot like mourning. Odds are it won't be entire. He will still sneak a listen on his own terms, alone, in the solipsistic pose of a boy in headphones, remembering how the beloved album had once belonged only to him.

By the time I reached college, *Ten* was blaring out of every dorm room. I was forced to share the album with strangers, jukeboxes, passing cars, cover bands, middle school girls, parents, high school thugs, and college yahoos. The lowest common denominator loved *Ten*, just as they had loved *Nevermind*.

My secret had lasted maybe six or eight months, although its status as a genuine secret is a bit dubious. No one had any intention of keeping *Ten* a secret. Nothing unpredictable happened. Nirvana was not the terminus of grunge, but its whetting stone. Seattle became a movement and people like movements. Epic, owned and operated by Sony BMG, was in the business of marketing and making money. They had the infrastructure to sell as many albums as the public demanded.

My biggest mistake in thinking I possessed a genuine secret and that Pearl Jam would elude Nirvana's exposure and retain its early cult status was my impression that *Ten* contained within it an immunity to ubiquity, an inherent contrariness to popularity. The "weird new music" that thrills the initiate and makes others shake their heads in disbelief does not describe the music of *Ten. Ten* was not Sonic Youth's *Daydream Nation* or Neutral Milk Hotel's *In the Aeroplane over the Sea* or Okkervil River's *Black Sheep Boy*—albums possessed of a kind of inscrutable brilliance that I'd argue fit the definition of Schopenhauer's "excellent work of art": "The noblest productions of genius must eternally remain sealed books to the dull majority of men, and are inaccessible to them. They are separated from them by a wide gulf, just as the society of princes is inaccessible to the common people." *Ten* was immediately accessible and quickly assimilated. There was nothing exclusive to me about the album's appeal. Others heard in Eddie Vedder's voice what I heard. The songs on *Ten* made them react as I had reacted.

Which is not to suggest that it didn't have a particular kind of brilliance. All that I admired about the album still applied. I just had the misfortune of being under the illusion of having discovered it. I should have realized that if the album had already penetrated the Chicago suburbs, I was a part of the tidal wave, and not a part of the shifting seabed that prompts the wave.

Still, when that illusion gave way, I reacted like the outrider burned by the broadening fan base. The most important musical discovery of my high school years rapidly turned into the same mall rock that I'd come to despise and that had spurred the restlessness that began my search out of mall rock.

I didn't know how to listen to *Ten* after that. How do you listen to an intimate piece of music turned into a phenomenon? I didn't know how to defend it to friends I made in college who wanted to dismiss it on the basis of its popularity alone. I lost the ability to talk about it. How do you talk to a casual listener tapping happily along to a song piped in from the café speakers, when you once worshipped that song? How do you greet the sight of someone on the campus shuttle flipping through liner notes that you once pored over with an emotion like piety?

I felt a loss when *Ten* became popular, a loss the nature of which I've struggled to articulate, in part because I think it must be a silly feeling, though no less genuine for that. The closest I can get is an exaggerated analogy. Imagine the Native American who refuses to have his picture taken out of fear of losing his soul, suddenly discovering his mug on the cover of *Time* magazine. *Ten* was very close to me, yet suddenly it was everywhere, so that when Eddie Vedder was seen howling into a mic on the cover of the October 25, 1993, issue of *Time*, when grunge was sold in the malls and paraded on runways and appearing in the photo shoots of glossy magazines, and the detractors were out and the parodies were forming and the imitators were warming up, I felt like something very close to me had been stolen.

* * *

Even as "Alive" swirled all around, as impossible to escape that season as "Smells Like Teen Spirit" had been the year before, I affected a pose of ignorance and indifference, in the spirit of the outrider.

But that doesn't mean I gave it up. I did the headphones thing, and it felt like mourning. Pearl Jam's sophomore album was released at midnight on the University of Iowa campus, but I was not among those who stood in line. I did buy it the next day, however, and I took that underground, too. Whether the shallow mindset of the outrider had warped my musical intuition, or whether *Versus* wasn't very good, either way I didn't take to it. More than likely, it had a hard time living up to *Ten*.

One should always aim to be the initiate, with the initiate's eye-bulging enthusiasm, but without any streak of the elitism that forecloses support for a good band simply because it's popular. A discriminating taste is a necessary and good thing, but if the tastemaker balks on stupid principle, the result is petty protest. Petty protest is ultimately self-restricting. Let's contain multitudes if we are to be true music lovers. I flip from Gang of Four to Garth Brooks with one click of the iPod wheel. I listen to both with frequency and affection. What do I care that one is sloganeering Brit post-punk and the other a populist country singer who distributes exclusively through Wal-Mart? They do different things for me at different times and I'm happy to have an appreciation of "Anthrax" and "Rodeo" both.

But I had to learn that lesson, and there had to be a sacrifice. There are albums I return to over and again because they continue to beguile, enchant, challenge, or thrill me. Others I listen to because they return me to a time and place. *Ten* I almost never listen to. Its enchantment was sapped, and playing it now only evokes a private loss. It was stolen from me because I allowed it to be stolen, but it was stolen all the same. I can't go back. I miss it. I miss the rush, I miss the intimacy. It got me out of the trenches. It was a matter of life or death. Now it's only an idle reminder, a symbol, not unlike a tombstone.

# I LOVE TO LISTEN TO

**10**

Eurythmics: *Savage* (Arista Records, 1987)
## Daniel Handler

If I tell you that the Eurythmics album *Savage* profoundly changed my life it'll seem like a joke. Put aside for the moment all of the inarguable albums one could put in that slot, the *Sgt. Peppers* and the *Kind of Blues* and the *It Takes a Nation of Millions to Hold Us Backs*. Assume for the sake of some strange argument that I had to limit myself to British electropop duos from roughly the same heyday and I'd be on much more serious ground with the Pet Shop Boys' *Introspective* or Orchestral Manoeuvres in the Dark's *Dazzle Ships* or Soft Cell's *Non-Stop Erotic Cabaret*, or, while we're on the word "cabaret," Cabaret Voltaire's *The Covenant, the Sword and the Arm of the Lord*, all of which at least have the technical and conceptual cred to merit consideration. Or I could jump back to my side of the pond, to Suicide's self-titled debut or Sparks's *In Outer Space*, a basically perfect album, and then maybe it wouldn't seem like a joke.

Also, there's the autobiographical angle: I could make a straightforward, nostalgic case for Yazoo's *Upstairs at Eric's* or Everything but the Girl's *Idlewild*, and tell you a story about the turntable, the birthday party, the night air through the window when her parents weren't home, the good coffee and the bad theft, the Japanese noodle place and the jaded joy and tedious terror of realizing it was never going to get better. None of that seems like a joke. I have good stories about They Might Be Giants's *Lincoln*, Julie London's *Lonely Girl*, Tom Waits's *Bone Machine*, the Clash's *Sandinista!*, and the Magnetic Fields's *69 Love Songs*, but I don't know if I can say those albums changed me. I certainly changed while those albums played, but the albums themselves are just pegs on which to hang stories, and in many cases the pegs don't matter. I could tell you all about the woman who used to call and leave songs from *Sunshine on Leith* on my answering machine, but the Proclaimers are just a placeholder in that story. When you're seventeen you can drive around at midnight listening to anything and your life will change. You will quit your job or your lover, dance with someone or miss them, see someone for the first time or the last time, realize that you're not alone or you are, that you're connected or dis-, that you aren't the person you thought you were, or it turns out you are, or someone else is or nobody is or everybody, which means the world isn't fair and life isn't worthwhile or it is and it is, and all the while it's a classic or an obscurity, a gem or an embarrassment, cred or poseur, *Ocean Beach* or *Ocean Rain*, *Giant Steps* or *Little Creatures*, *OK Computer*, *Computer World*, *The Freewheelin' Suzanne Vega*, *Achtung Baby It's Cold Outside*, and then it begins to seem like a joke after all.

I don't want to tell you one of those stories, because this album didn't change my life in a moment of personal crisis or epiphany. *Savage* has changed my life more like a book changes lives: slowly, purposefully, insidiously, it has altered my worldview, strengthened certain suspicions and instincts and knocked others off the shelf. It has actually altered my stance. I live according to its principles. It was a moment of personal crisis and epiphany, all by itself, all twelve tracks.

Eurythmics's *Savage*? A joke, right?

Eurythmics were, and sort of are, the duo of Annie Lennox and Dave Stewart. They derive their name from a term I've never understood, from the time I first looked it up in sixth grade to sitting right here at my desk with volume five of the *Oxford English Dictionary*: "A system of rhythmical bodily movements, esp. dancing exercises, with musical accompaniment, freq. used for educational purposes." Um, what? In any case, they had a first album nobody heard, and then hit it big with "Sweet Dreams (Are Made of This)." You've heard this song. There's one synthesizer riff over and over and a few lines of world-weary philosophy in the lyrics, and then the band rattles a few milk bottles and the thing fades out with a few improvised wails. I remember hearing it on the radio in junior high school, wondering what in the world it was. It sounded like a gospel choir and yet also like a low-budget science fiction television show.

This was a balancing act the band kept working, keeping one foot on the cold, inscrutable surfaces of electropop and the other in the heartfelt depths of soul, and at the time these contradictions seemed pretty daring and delicious. This was also the era of prime MTV, so the band played around visually as well. There's the "Here Comes the Rain Again" video, in which Lennox wanders the beach while Stewart stalks her with a video camera, possibly making the video she's starring in, and "Who's That Girl?" in which a spurned Lennox is romanced by an Elvis impersonator, also played by Lennox, so that at the end of the video she's kissing herself. Or "herself." Or something. The questions these videos seem to be asking are the arch and obvious ones over which the early 1980s kept raising its eyebrows. It was a time when "Is Boy George gay?" seemed like a dizzying and provocative query.

But in a few years that query was very easily answered with "Of course Boy George is gay—look at him," and similarly, Eurythmics lost their cred. They made a couple of straight soul albums that are lovely but unconvincing, even in their hits: "Would I Lie To You?" has insincerity right there in the title, and "Missionary Man" doesn't even make the obvious, sexual joke required of a soul song called "Missionary Man," and nonsexualized insincerity is pretty much the opposite of soul music, and there it went out the window. The band was still popular—some halfhearted research kept putting the stat "75 million records" on my screen—but somehow they were never really cool again. They're still not cool. They're not cool in an obscure way, like Visage or Dexy's Midnight Runners, and they're not cool in a familiar way, like Elvis Costello or David Bowie, and they're not cool in an underground way, like Joy Division or the Smiths, and they're not even so uncool that they're cool, like Wham! or the Thompson Twins. They have no cred. They have no soul cred. They have no electronic cred. They have no new wave cred. They hang out on VH1 now and then, but they don't even seem to be the part of '80s nostalgia in which people want to wallow—that is, they're not cool even when you think about the time they used to be cool.

I never stopped loving them, but that's not what I'm trying to say here.

*Savage* was released at a particular low point, cred-wise, for Eurythmics. It's the other album nobody heard. Continuing my halfhearted research I Googled "favorite album is Eurythmics' *Savage*" and got nothing. I Googled "favorite album is *Savage*" and got one hit, one other guy who liked this album best: Dave Stewart of Eurythmics. The other Eurythmic, Annie Lennox, doesn't look like she likes it much. She's pouting and rolling her eyes on the cover, with long shiny nails and a cheap wig not quite 100 percent straight. It looks like you've paid for her time but not for her attention. She's heavily made up, with gaudy eyes and lined lips and a dabbed-on beauty mark. It's a trashy look, but carefully trashy, reminding me of something Dolly Parton said: "You'd be surprised how much it costs to look this cheap." The photography itself is gorgeous: sepia-toned with an almost gelatin depth, an Ansel Adams portrait of a harlot; inside the booklet, the wig has slipped further, so you can see Lennox's real hair underneath, a much darker shade. The record company even shelled out for a "video album," that is, music videos for all twelve songs, in which this Dolly dame bumps up against hausfraus, leather queens, peasant girls, and rock stars, all played by Lennox and all looking fake.

The fakeness is deliberate, of course—a deliberate slip from something already deliberate—but let's not drag this into academic territory. The look is not an inquiry into identity. It's not a take on female beauty, or the manipulation of mass media. Maybe if the album were called *Drag* or *Woman* or *Like a Virgin* or *Blonde on Blonde*, the image would be some reference to the slippery nature of reality or the inevitable exploitation inherent in commercial imagery. The "Who's That Girl?" video asked "Who's that girl?" and answered it with a woman dressed as a man kissing a woman dressed as another woman. But the cover of *Savage* doesn't lead to any such thing. It doesn't look savage, for instance, or the opposite of savage, and it's too beautiful to be mocking beauty. Basically it looks gussied-up and tarty, and then it makes sure you know that they know it's gussied-up and tarty. It's an amuse-bouche of irony that folds in on itself for no reason except to engage and amuse.

In other words, it's a joke.

The album opens with "Beethoven (I Love to Listen To)," one of a select group of songs the titles of which have a parenthetical suffix containing a textual prefix, most famously Adam Ant's "Physical (You're So)." In the world anyone would do this (Who knows why)? It begins with the bonk-bonk-bonk of a drum machine under several bars of what sounds like an airplane engine, the album's only discernible similarity with the Beatles' "White Album," the pitch getting higher and higher, building and building, and I can remember my first listen. I bought *Savage* on cassette at a crappy record store, long out of business, down the street from work. I was seventeen and my job was piano accompanist for the Congregation Sherith Israel Youth Choir, every Sunday morning, bleary from Saturday night with my girlfriend, sightreading D-minor vamps for misbehaving youngsters warbling Hebrew, and more often than not I bought a tape for the ride home in my mother's '65 Mustang, which I parked illegally in the hospital parking lot. I ripped open the cellophane wrapping with my car keys and left it glittering on the passenger seat, tipped open the case with the hand that wasn't on the steering wheel, and threw the tape into the player. And then heard this, as I engined down the hill of California Street, the beat thunking, the airplane pitch rising, rising, rising, and finally clattering into the song, but there it is, the autobiographical angle, because what song wouldn't have sounded good like that?

The airplane fades away and there are more drums. Or "drums"—the only guest musician credited is one Olle Romo, responsible for "all programming"—making the same blank noises over and over, and synthesizers too, and when Lennox comes in even she sounds programmed, singing bits of the parenthetical over and over: "I love to / I love to / I love to / I love to / I love to / Listen to / I love to / Listen to." When the verse kicks in, it's double-tracked, with one Annie Lennox singing and the other one talking more or less the same lyrics, pitching a hypothetical song—"Take a girl like that, and put her in a natural setting, like a café for example. Along comes the boy, and he's looking for trouble . . ."—until we're back at "I love to / Listen to / I love to / Listen to," and finally, the word "Beethoven." What are they talking about? What do they mean? In passionate if mannered voices, the Lennoxes seem to be describing a song they can't bother to sing, and then admitting that they'd actually prefer classical music. In the second verse, they're talking in arch first person: "Did I tell you I was lying, by the way?" and at the third verse Lennox just laughs, the showy, braying laugh of a soap opera vixen finally getting her revenge. "Beethoven," repeat and fade.

Now, the point isn't that it doesn't make any sense. A great deal of music doesn't make any sense. Even a music lover of unspeakably varied taste will find a genre or two completely elusive, and pop music probably makes the least amount of sense, from "Louie Louie" to "a mosquito, my libido." You're not supposed to know why Bob Dylan's blues resemble that of Tom Thumb or why Prince only wants to see you bathing in the purple rain. But when I listen to *Savage* I hear a different game. Its nonsense isn't a throwback to preliterate pop like "A whop bop a loo bop a whop bam boom," or an arty, modernist conceit like "The reflex is an only child, he's waiting in the park," and it's not delineating a subculture, as with the Pet Shop Boys or the Wu Tang Clan, in which getting what's really going on is part of the listen. It's ironic, certainly, but it's not the sort of irony we're used to, even in this age, when Ween plays a country and western song in order to make fun of the genre and of itself, or Señor Coconut does a mambo version of a Kraftwerk song to find a sweaty groove inside an automated one, and vice versa. It's something else. The verses of "I've Got a Lover (Back in Japan)" praise the lover in question while the chorus shouts "Break, break, break away those ties"; "Do You Want to Break Up?" doesn't just refuse a yes or no answer, but muddles things even further, Lennox implying that she's hoping for one answer, expecting another, dreading the answer she hopes for and then expecting the dread, but cataloging the twists and turns only takes away from the utter trashiness of what you're actually hearing. "You Have Placed a Chill in My Heart" contains the lines:

*I'll be the figure of your disgrace*
*A crisscross pattern upon your face*
*A woman's just too tired to think*
*About the dirty old dishes in the kitchen sink*

which maybe look arty and forbidding on the page but on the stereo are just catchy. They have the offhand juxtaposition and vague specificity of the folk songs from what Greil Marcus calls "the old, weird America," a description that also sounds arty and forbidding but turns out to describe music that you might have sung at summer camp, such as Clarence "Tom" Ashley's "The Coo Coo Bird," a song on Harry Smith's famed *Anthology of American Folk Music*:

> *Gonna build me a log cabin on a mountain so high*
> *So I can see Willie as he goes on by*
> *Oh the coo coo is a pretty bird, she wobbles when*
>     *she flies*
> *She never hollers coo coo 'til the fourth day of July.*

It's sacrilege, I know, to compare the unknowable depths of the foundations of American music to an ignored album by a synthpop duo: the cred gap is simply too wide. The lyrics of "The Coo Coo Bird," cool people would tell us, have a genuine insensibility; one imagines Ashley learned them at the knee of some elder, who adapted and/or muddled them as part of the great game of Telephone, the way such music was transmitted in a culture unattached to mechanical recording or even written records. With "You Have Placed a Chill in My Heart," on the other hand, the lyrics and music are written and recorded under the auspices of corporate enterprise. Therefore that weird quatrain is a different kind of weird, a fake weird, a put-on weird, a joke.

Which is precisely what *Savage* kept telling me from the first time I heard it until the listens that have guided this essay. It's joking, and the jokes themselves build a new platform and dig a new depth. The lyrics don't just follow a train of thought so distant that one is encouraged to participate in making sense of them; they keep on telling you that this train of thought is constructed both carefully and carelessly. *Savage* presents a world with the seams showing, on purpose, and with the seams of making the seams showing showing. It catapults past homage, camp, and satire into a new real thing, even though it's fake. Or, as Lennox sings in the next song:

> *Now there's a lifestyle with painted lips*
> *Now there's a lifestyle, everybody wants it but it*
>     *don't exist*

Or, in the title track that closes side one, "Everything is fiction," although this lyric is preceded by "She said," part of a shifting portrait of an unreliable woman sung by an unreliable woman. Who is she? Haven't the faintest. Who's that Willie guy going by the cabin?

The music reflects this unreliability, complicating the balancing act between electronics and soul not just by having one play against the other—they've always done that—but by admitting both are put-ons. The album has a groove that rarely lets up, but it never stops reminding you that a groove is basically the same thing repeated over and over, and that the excitement it creates is largely a projection. Side two opens with "I

Need a Man," the closest thing to a hit found on *Savage*. We hear some clattery drums, either electronic or treated to sound electronic, and then Lennox says, "Hey! Is it my turn? You want me to sing now? Okay." But there's no way this is studio chatter, caught when Lennox thought she was off-mic—it's delivered in a bellowing Deep South growl, a far cry from the Brit's real voice. A song from another album released around the same time, Sting's *The Dream of the Blue Turtles*, opens with a band member asking "What key is it in?" and it's irritating: we're being asked to believe that a carefully produced pop album was actually tossed off by musicians who hadn't rehearsed. With Lennox, you know she's faking, and she knows you know she's faking, and then she launches into the most passionate vocal on the album, an utterly convincing lusty romp, undercut continually by that opening bit of stagecraft. Probably my favorite musical moment on the album is toward the end of "Put the Blame on Me." Lennox purrs, "Tell the one that's lying with you to get right up and go back home," and then for the rest of the song, a full two minutes, "Get right up / And go back home" is repeated in the background. But for some reason the electronic backing basically skips a bar, and so for the emphasis to sync up the band has to cheat a little, and for one moment "Get right up" and "and go back home" play at the same time. If you're singing along you're suddenly one line behind. Recorded music is full of these odd, imperfect moments—the dropped beat on a jazz record, one string on a blues guitar suddenly ringing wrong—but Eurythmics have arranged for this to happen. It took effort. You'd be surprised how much effort it took to sound this cheap.

The album largely abandons electronics in the finish, winding down with "I Need You," an acoustic song in which the album's most obvious lyrics ("I need you to listen to the ecstasy I'm faking / I'm faking / I'm faking / I'm faking / I need you") are nearly drowned out by the sound of an audience talking, laughing, clinking glasses—doing anything but listening, and *Savage* closes with "Brand New Day," which serves as testament to how thoroughly the album's trickery has messed with my brain. It's basically a straight-up gospel song, but because of everything that's come before it I always wait, every time I hear it, for a punch line. Out of context the song would sound like a sincere if corny message of hope. That could even be what it is. But after everything else, a sincere statement sounds ten times more fake than all of the pretension that has preceded it.

And that's really how *Savage* changed my life, by presenting irony and showmanship as honesty and truth until honesty and truth without irony and showmanship look less honest and untruthful. The album hit me in adolescence, when I was going through the usual tumult of realizing that the world isn't what it says it is, and that the truths we're all told aren't truths after all, and much wonderful music has been made complaining about this or ignoring it or triumphing in spite of it. But *Savage*, instead, triumphs because of it. The album told me that truth could be a part of this world of fakery, that irony and game-playing weren't a way of avoiding or confronting the world but a way of living in it, that a hall of mirrors can actually present an accurate reflection. There are lots of other ways to learn this, of course—it's why I like Voltaire better than Tolstoy, and Baudelaire better than Frost; it's why a great article in the *Onion* can provide more political insight than an op-ed piece in the *New York Times*. The next generation learned it from Beck, who announces and mocks himself as a B-boy, a lady-killer, a cowboy, a robot, and a folk hero, all with genuine jokey aplomb. But *Savage* was what tilted the world for me, and it's what continues to do it, because its statement about the world's cred is all the more powerful from a document that has no cred whatsoever. *Savage* wasn't cool, but I listened to *Savage* anyway, and realized that I didn't have to decide between anger at the world and jadedness at my anger, between joy and the self-consciousness that surrounds joy, between losing my cred and keeping my cool, because they're all actually the same thing. It's no wonder, sometime around my gazillionth listen to the album, that I ended up becoming a fiction writer—and, I can add with a roll of my eyes, a truth teller.

There are those who might see this as a hipster's manifesto, another example of a media-addled lost soul finding more meaning in some forgotten piece of pop trash than in genuine, worthwhile culture. Certainly there are no tracks on *Savage* that could be listed with the work of great songwriters, but as much joy as recognizably great music has brought me, I'm not sure it has changed me—or you. Unless you never would have ended up who you are—a bass player, maybe, or a critical biographer—because of a certain piece of music, then any album you heard is just another arrow in your emotional quiver, another peg for your autobiography, another artist strutting and fretting on the stage in front of you. *Savage* showed me that the whole world was the stage, that every image was calculated, that everything was fiction, but that was no reason to get right up and go back home. I learned, and still learn, from *Savage* that it's not necessary to tone down one's gimlet glance to see the world as it is, that looking askance at things is in fact the best way to look at them directly. The joy and fury of the world, like the joy and fury of music, burns just as brightly whether you are listening to Beethoven or a woman cackling about listening to Beethoven. It's a joke, yes, but what isn't a joke? And the thing with jokes is that I love to listen to them.

# 11
# AM I GETTING WARMER?

The B-52s: *The B-52s* (Warner Bros. Records, 1979)
### Clifford Chase

WINTER 1980

Upper quad was a clearing in the redwoods, lower quad a knoll overlooking the ocean; I lived in lower quad, in Dorm Eight.

With some pride I put on my surplus khakis and the white button-down shirt I had discovered in a box at my parents' house over Christmas break—my new look.

That fall I had cut my hair for the first time since high school, and grown my first beard.

Between the two quads lay a courtyard and the dining hall, which also overlooked the ocean; by the steps was a white stucco wall covered in bougainvillea, which bloomed year-round.

• • •

I seem to be describing a prehistoric time—crucial but shrouded.

It was my senior year.

As the brand-new record strummed its cockeyed beat, I stared at the five of them on the cover: angular cutouts on a flat, horizonless yellow—three boys, two girls—defiant in their thrift-shop clothes and poofy wigs.

Journal entry: "Legitimate (I think) fears and desires concerning my sexuality are taking the form of guilt."

Remembering that time requires extra kindness toward myself.

I spooned fuchsia-colored yogurt from the plastic tub.

Under a vaulted timber ceiling, I pulled the heavy blue *Canterbury Tales* from the shelf marked with the course number.

Let the white space between these sentences stand for what couldn't be seen then; or what can't be remembered now; or my open fate; or the open, bare-bones arrangement of a B-52s song (drum kit, guitar, cheesy keyboard, toy piano).

"The person who is writing this journal is perhaps on his way out," I wrote.

• • •

I walked toward some dark trees in the dry yellow light under a pale turquoise cloudless sky.

Particular tension of standing with my tray on the edge of the dining hall, deciding whom to sit with.

My friends: (1) Every night at about nine, Cathy came up to my room with the backgammon board and I pulled our favorite record from its bright yellow jacket. (2) Like me, Chris had sandy blond hair, a light brown beard, and glasses, and he covered his mouth and looked sideways when he laughed, as if, also like me, he dwelt perpetually in high school study hall. (3) Ellie—peripheral then; central later—was "intensely neurotic," I wrote to a friend. (4) I've known Mike since I was twelve, so describing him is like describing the air.

"And also, now that [my brother] Ken is gay," my journal continues, "I have lost one more person to identify with. I used to imitate him quite a bit, I think. But now that is impossible, unless I want to be gay."

Though I wrote "now that"—as if the event were recent—Ken had come out to me almost a year earlier.

The beeping at the start of "Planet Claire": signal from some distant part of myself.

Cathy's short, blond hair, thick glasses, and slightly crossed brown eyes; her husky-fluty Peppermint Patty laughter.

• • •

I sat alone in the sunshine on last year's tall dry grass, below which new grass had sprouted with the rain and was already a few inches tall.

I made a pen and ink drawing of a cluster of trees.

Mike and I ran side by side down the rocky path—pleasure of my feet hitting the earth, in rhythm with his.

The campus was spread across hills and ravines of redwoods, bay trees, the occasional maple, live oaks, ferns, and vast stretches of tall waving grass—emerald in winter, golden the rest of the year.

In the professor's office I recitcd the opening of *The Canterbury Tales*, in Middle English, enjoying the oddsounding yet familiar words on my tongue and in my throat.

We received narrative evaluations instead of grades (a grand 1960s experiment, later abandoned), and stringy-haired guys sold pot out of gigantic black garbage bags in their dorm rooms.

I was attending the stoner school of all time and I didn't even like pot.

When Chris encountered any sort of falseness or stupidity, he said "Ew" in a quick, guttural way that reminded me I had found a fellow traveler in disgust.

• • •

The year before, I had decided the people in the campus Christian group I belonged to were creeps, and I left the group.

I began saying "Ew" exactly as Chris did, and soon Cathy did, too.

I almost never sat with Cathy in the dining hall; I saw her almost exclusively at night, in the dorm.

I was in the process of forming myself, as if from nothing, from what was available—my classes, my records, my second-hand clothes, my new friends and our running jokes, my letters to and from old friends—as if from popsicle sticks, tin foil, and yarn.

To explain Middle English pronunciation to Ellie, I recast a Michael Jackson song as "Ee lavah the way ye shakah yourrr thingah."

The closet as a kind of innocence.

In Chaucer I was learning to distinguish the teller and his limitations from the tale itself.

"The sturdy and flamboyant Wife of Bath finds herself at a transitional time of life," I wrote.

Though I wasn't a Christian anymore, I still believed viscerally in things like demon possession and the notion that certain actions inevitably bring punishment.

• • •

Piercing retro sci-fi organ of "There's a Moon in the Sky."

I have little memory of those evenings with Cathy, as if our study breaks took place beyond the long arm of self-consciousness.

My grandmother's crazy quilt beneath the backgammon board.

The click of dice and checkers, the crackle of the record player.

Cathy and I were barely more than acquaintances then and couldn't have known we were also knitting a lifelong friendship.

We never danced, instead playing quietly like good children, occasionally bouncing a foot to the quirky tunes.

Screechy guitar. Fred Schneider shouting, "HELLO?" We laughed. More screechy guitar. "HELLO?"

Outside my dorm room window—moonlight, redwoods, the open dry fields descending to the ocean.

In the cool morning air I crossed a ravine on the footbridge, shaded by bay trees.

In the clothing store in Monterey, the clerk asked if I was in a fraternity. I said no, we didn't have fraternities at Santa Cruz. He seemed disappointed, I tried on a sport coat. He stood behind me grazing my butt with his fingers, explaining that that was exactly where the jacket should fall.

Slashing guitar sets up pleasure in my throat, a sensation identified by the writer Wayne Koestenbaum with regard to the opera fan, but I think it applies to all musical enjoyment—a silent, sympathetic hum in the vocal cords.

"I'm afraid again tonight that there is so much keeping me from ever having a sexual relationship," I wrote in my journal. "I keep allowing myself to . . . laugh at a certain moment, turn my head at a certain moment, etc.—to diffuse sexuality."

Cathy liked to imitate the way the girls sang "Jackie O," the percussive k, the long o.

I tried to think about women when I masturbated and often succeeded.

"But the Wife of Bath has expressed earlier an almost despairing awareness of the intractability of her own spirit, which is unwilling to restrain its 'immoral' impulses."

Were my professors perhaps moved by how lost I was?

The guy with washboard abs playing Ping-Pong; the hairy-chested guy riding his skateboard in and out of the quad; the poet-mathematician who lingered in my dorm room one night and I didn't know why; the guy who wore shorts all winter, who invited me into his dorm room, shut the door, and lay there grinning at me through his sparse but attractive beard, and I didn't know why.

"Dance this mess around."

The paved path skirted a dry, sunny hillside.

I'm trying to grasp the nature of dreaming and living despite myself.

Wet Speedo of a professor hanging to dry on the casement window of his office.

Periodically Cathy and I tried to parse this odd, ironic kind of music that was totally new to us—playful, nostalgic, assembled from junk and nonsense.

We misidentified the opening *Peter Gunn* riff as James Bond, though this correctly located the sound in childhood memories of sexiness, swank, and intrigue, as seen on TV.

We decided that the planet where people had no heads was San Jose, the endless suburb where Cathy, too, had grown up.

The one out gay student I knew seemed to dwell on the outside of everything—I always saw him sitting alone in the same spot, on bare concrete, his back against the rough concrete wall, rolling a cigarette.

I lay in bed with a cold, my fourth that year.

Dream: "A vague sex scene of great passion. I am avoiding saying that I kissed his ass, and that it was extremely smooth and muscular and white. . . . I was in a sense a different person—fear and conscience and guilt siphoned off. Except . . . I think my mother was there."

The year before, after the gay grad student moved out of the dorm, the stoners claimed to have found a jar of Vaseline under his bed.

I ran alone through the dry scrub and woods.

I stopped to say hi to a girl from the dorm named Patty. She said, "You look cute in your running shorts." "With these skinny arms?" I asked, lifting them. She shook her head. "It's the whole *package*, Cliff." I ran on.

These ideas about myself, in the forest of myself.

I hadn't even kissed a girl (or anyone) since I was fourteen.

In "There's a Moon in the Sky," Fred assured me that if I felt like a misfit, there were, in fact, "thousands of others like you! Others like you!" and since he didn't specify what those others were, I didn't have to be afraid.

• • •

Queer child looks up at the night sky, in search of sympathy.

"Ellie and I and Chris and another guy slept outside last Friday night," I wrote in my journal. "Ellie and I stayed up talking, and reality began to fade. She began to say how no one was ever attracted to her. So I (fearfully) said that I didn't consider our friendship as entirely Platonic. . . . She said, 'Well, thanks. I think you're attractive too.' I felt brushed aside."

We woke surrounded by cows.

I wrote, "Perhaps I need to allow myself to be a fool, to fail, to cease analyzing, to get drunk, to make a pass. . . . How does romance 'happen'?"

I arranged to have a picnic with Marya, a girl I knew from my dorm the previous year.

We lay on a blanket in a field and I was almost attracted to her—her white round face and long peasant skirt.

It's as if my own desire were a doll—I was always trying to make it do things, act out a story, sit or stand or pretend to walk.
Marya and I talked "deeply," there on the grass in the sun, but then we folded up the blanket and walked back to the dorms without even a kiss.

• • •

I wrote of "The Nun's Priest's Tale": "The Priest also appears quite interested in the problem of 'vanitee,' in a broad sense of the word as inadequate and illusory ways of thinking (and speaking) that inevitably deceive and prejudice us."

Fred Schneider's unsuccessful attempt to call a number written on the bathroom wall—"I dial stupid number ALL DAY LONG!"

Journal: "I had set a goal for myself to become sexually involved with someone before I graduate. I would have few regrets about UCSC if that happened. . . ."

It seems as though Cathy and I spent many months playing backgammon and listening to records but actually it was only a single quarter, just ten weeks.

"The principle girls of the USA," followed by a list of names: my introduction to pop art.

Motown fragments in "Dance This Mess Around": my introduction to pastiche.

"Ska-doo-da-bop—Eeww": delight or disgust?

The enigma of "Rock Lobster": my introduction to nonsense, and its importance.

Cathy graduated; I had one more term to go.

• • •

## Spring 1980

For as long as I can remember, I have castigated myself for not properly enjoying things, first toys, later people, moments, and landscapes.

No record or memory of what I did over spring break.

Patch of pale blue ocean in the distance, which I always tried to appreciate as lovely and serene, but which mostly seemed to disappear in my mind.

The stoners sat shirtless in front of the dorm; constant snickering and hacking and mulling over "buds" and "sinsemilla"; continual drone of Pink Floyd, speakers pointed out the window.

I was indeed lost to myself and on myself and yet I was also completely myself, as much as any weird prehistoric creature was itself, if doomed, if purely transitional on the evolutionary ladder, completely itself and utterly unseen, except for the fossil, a kind of shadow across time.

Chris and I jumped over the four-foot wall that everyone jumped over to get to the mailboxes.

It was beautiful everywhere you looked: bright gold poppies appeared in all the fields, and wisteria draped the walkways of the college next to mine.

I sat on a bench in the sunshine reading my evaluations.

My Chaucer professor praised my "detailed familiarity with the text" as well as my "hard work and keen intelligence."

I enrolled in his course on Spenser's *Faerie Queene.*

The fiction teacher let me into her workshop because I said I liked Flannery O'Connor.

"Let the games begin," said Chris, imitating a creature on *Star Trek*, and he pretended to click his alien fingers. "Khee! Khee!"

Cathy came to visit for a few days, before moving to New York; she slept on the floor of my dorm room.

"I finally got up the nerve to ask her to sleep with me. She was out of the sleeping bag on the floor and into the bed in a second. I got scared though. We kissed and held each other. I was shaking. Eventually I relaxed though. We couldn't have intercourse because she had no protection. . . . I never came. . . . We laughed a lot and made jokes while we were making love. . . . Finally we just went to sleep. . . . I felt like I had gone as far as I wanted . . . such a shock, really, to make love, to be naked, to sleep with another . . . the night was awful. I couldn't sleep. . . . I felt so boxed in with her sleeping beside me, in the narrow bed. . . . In the morning we made love a bit more. . . . She seemed to be doing the wrong thing. I just felt rubbed and wiggled. . . . She would breath in my ear and lick it and I would practically go wild. But when she tried to make me come, I couldn't."

Fred yelling "having fun!"—either forced, manic enjoyment or enraged sarcasm.

Mike asked, "Well, Cliff, wasn't it pleasurable?"

I started seeing a counselor at the university's health center.

Now that Cathy was gone, I listened to the B-52's by myself.

Cindy or Kate going "wild" over her idol, growling, screeching—

At breakfast I overheard someone say the super muscular guy from Dorm Six had freaked out on acid, and it took several people to hold him down; I feigned disinterest, stirring my burned granola.

The cafeteria overlooked grassy hills rolling down to the distant bay, like a restaurant in a National Park.

I lay in bed with another bad cold, my fingers grazing the short, brown, napless carpet.

Dream: "[My brother] Ken's arm was cut off. He was acting strangely, down and out. . . . He said his supervisor pulled at his arm and it came off. . . . [Later] Mom sent me a letter saying something like, 'I no longer curse fate. My rebellious children are mutilated, slain, ill . . .'"

I policed everything I thought and said but occasionally let slip a telling lie: of Mike's red-haired roommate, I said, "His hair is the most amazing color. What I want to know is, does he have a sister?"

Looking back at myself then is a little like watching *Mr. Magoo*.

Mike was tall, with dirty-blond hair that curled on his shoulders, gray eyes, a wide face, and aquiline nose.

Regarding psychotherapy: "I feel so ugly, bleeding, exposed. And I need to be exposed. The rationalizations are fading. . . . Greg said I have to come down from the mountain and be part of the human race. . . . I feel so ugly, so juvenile, so wrong, wrong, wrong. . . .

". . . letting go, losing control, being ugly, bloody, gaping, awkward, driven, limp-wristed, ineffectual, but whole, alive, washed raw or something. But still I don't cry. . . . I sweat instead of crying. After a session with Greg I'm drenched. . . . Pressure about my eyes, sweat pouring out my armpits. I go through 2 or 3 shirts a day, my brow is furrowed a lot, and I look at the ground as I walk."

• • •

My ability to see myself clearly, and my ability to fool myself.

"Unraveling. That is what I want. Let it all unravel."

The campus teemed with slender young men and women in shorts and T-shirts, yet sometimes in my memory the place seems stark and empty—blank, sunny expanses of white stucco or concrete or open fields, as schematic as the island of retired spies in *The Prisoner.*

"Sweat, sleep, eat, shit."

Voices outside my door, in the hall: "Gnarly . . . Killer . . ."

In my room, Fred called: "Destination: Moon."

Saturday night I danced "wildly" with Ellie in the quad, to "Rock Lobster"; saw Marya watching from the stoop of her dorm, in her big owl-ly glasses; felt elation turn to regret.

The Rock Lobster—life of the party, or angry outsider?

"Everybody rockin'. Everybody fruggin' "—the perfect party, or outcast's nightmare?

Seeing the tragic in a B-52s song might be an aberrant reading, but so what.

• • •

I continued rereading the books on my list for my final oral exam, a requirement in my major.

"But that complexity and completeness that is holiness rests on the achievement of a level of human insight that is finally revealed by the poet to be a virtual impossibility," I wrote, of *The Faerie Queene*.

Possibility of sharing a place in San Francisco that summer with my high school friend Wayne, as we had done the previous summer in Berkeley.

Letter to another friend: "My friend Ellie has been telling me a lot about herself lately, and I'm always afraid that I will reject her."

I dreamed I compared cocks with the tall sexy preppy who lived upstairs.

I reread the *Iliad*.

I forced myself to get involved with Liz, a girl in my dorm.

It was a drought year; "If it's yellow, let it mellow . . ."

"I have been getting closer to Liz. . . . Mostly I like her because she listens to me so raptly. . . . When, when, when will I simply like someone and pursue them?"

No one could sound more milquetoast than Fred growling that his love is "erupting."

• • •

I was attempting a new kind of Houdini trick—letting only half myself out of my shell.

I reread Plato's *Apology*.

Day after day of sunshine and dry air; the hillsides were brown again by early May.

I wrote short stories about: the gay man who had been my boss at a summer job; an argument I had with Ellie; my mother's resentment toward my father; a sheriff whose brother loses his arm; my being chased by a bull, which I had dreamed.

The guy down the hall said to me, "Let's make a Liz sandwich," and I pretended to laugh.

The clear sky, the open horizon of the sea, and my amorphous inner blob of unhappiness, shame, frustration, rage, confusion.

The fiction teacher suggested my protagonist might be attracted to the character named Mike. I disagreed.

The odd nature of the closet, the open secret, not only to others but to oneself.

Periods of denial and periods of self-awareness.

• • •

"There's a moon in the sky. It's called the moon."

And yet by starting to write fiction that year, I had, in a way, already left Santa Cruz.

In the coed bathroom, after I had peed, Ellie said, in faux Southern accent, "I love a man with a strong urethra!"

In New York she would become my girlfriend, off and on, for three years—but that's another story.

I'm not describing a straight path toward anything, rather a series of windings.

"We're blessed, we're blessed, we're blessed, we're blessed," Chris sang one morning at breakfast, aping Tammy Faye Bakker.

As kids my brother Ken and I had often entertained each other with parody cartoons of bad TV dramas.

As far as I can tell, I barely spoke to Ken that year. Letter from my high school friend Wayne telling me he was gay.

He was involved with a guy in Cambridge, so he wouldn't be moving to San Francisco for the summer after all.

Reply to Wayne, admitting, "I, too, have had feelings toward men."

• • •

I heard Liz's voice out in the hall, but didn't go out to talk to her.

Music as relief from continually having to choose and choose and choose.

The cymbal rolls like a gong as Fred calls, "Down, down!"—submarine, fellator, dreamer.

I tried to decide where to move after graduation, if not San Francisco.

I wondered what it would be like to have sex with Wayne.

I flipped to the black page in *Tristram Shandy*.

Every twenty-two-year-old is lost in the effort of formation, but some more than others—more secretive, more fumbling, more "from scratch," more thwarted, more hopeless, more undaunted, more against-all-odds.

Chris broke out giggling at the slightest sign of humor, so he was constantly saying, "Sorry. Sorry. Go on."

Chris also turned out to be gay, but that was later.

I reread *Sir Gawain and the Green Knight*.

Liz told me she had never met anyone so sensitive.

• • •

The fear of exposure, the self-ridicule, the inward no-no-no, the ickiness, the closed loop, the hope that somehow I could be different, the forced blooms of hetero desire, the sheer effort of it all, the constant expenditure of mental and emotional energy.

"Can you name, name, name, name them today?" sang Kate and Cindy on the morning of my exam.

In the book-lined office I took my seat before the three professors—and froze.

I couldn't seem to answer any of their questions.

At one point I said, "Am I getting warmer?"

"He was, however, clearly nervous," said the evaluation, "and this led to a self-consciousness in his answers that produced a rather blocked exam. There was a disappointing tentativeness to his performance—though he knew his texts, he had trouble deploying them in the exam context. . . . When encouraged to develop a perspective he had thought through, he tended to lose the edge of his argument and become distracted and diffuse. . . . He managed to convey an ability he did not fully demonstrate."

Afterward, Mike comforted me over a beer.

Of Liz I wrote: "There is something missing—what is it?"

Whenever I told my therapist I might be gay, he threatened to send me to the gay counselor on staff.

Description of Liz: "She is Chinese. She has long hair, a face like a Gauguin. She is very insecure. But when we are just alone and talking, none of the negative matters."

Invitation from a friend in Texas to come live in Austin, where a guy she knew was making a movie that I could work on.

It all comes back to me like the details of a herky-jerky dream.

Describing a single B-52's song from start to finish would be like climbing inside a dream of my frustrated, secretive youth.

Regarding Liz: "I want to kiss her, I want to touch her. But there are blocks, blocks, BLOCKS. Obstacles."

"Can I ever stop pressuring myself to feel certain things?"

Tinny '60s organ, like some forgotten Morse code. "Remember," Cindy breathily confides, "when you held my hand." A succession of girl-group fragments. She's stuck in a world of clichés, seeking glamorous wisdom. I feel for Cindy—she's lost her man. The faint toy piano: generic scary-movie "insanity." At last the stock phrases give way to screams: "Why don't you dance with me? I'm not no limburger!" Comic but also kind of heartbreaking. She's only screaming like I wish I could. Fred chimes in now, the circus ringleader: "Dance this mess around!" Whipping up the animals, egging on the dream. The guitar insists, and now Kate tells of parties at which she, also a mess, is danced around in various styles—"shy tuna . . . camel walk . . . hippy shake." I, too, knew the hippy shake—it could still be seen at parties in Santa Cruz, circa 1980. I, too, a mess—though never so artfully described as by Kate's trumpet-y soprano, slightly raspy, almost screechy—singing the title sentence over and over, in ever wilder melodies, as if in madness or abandon, while the others sing their "yeahs"—affirmation at last?

A cute guy from the dorm told me he freaked out on acid and saw a giant grasshopper up in a field.

"All afternoon I was lying here trying to have a nap and feeling like I am breaking apart emotionally. Pressure on all sides: parents, school, myself, Liz, and finally my psychologist. For a moment I fell asleep, and a British voice said, 'Everyone accusing you. It's too much. Don't you think you need a pardon?'"

Fred's falsetto "British" accent: "Rock lobster?"

The phrase repeated over and over, as if it could mean anything—and does.

•  •  •

Another brief dream in which I wanted to saw my way across a bridge—destroying, going to a lot of trouble and turmoil for nothing, just to clear the way that was already clear.

"I wish my life would stop, so much happens. . . . I have been getting closer to Liz sexually. . . . I just looked out the window. It is a beautiful day—rainy, cloudy, some sun, and the grass is all brown. . . . I love rain and cold in summertime."

I considered staying in Santa Cruz for the summer; I wondered if Liz being there was a plus or a minus.

Regarding Liz: "So we got to the shirt-taking-off point, and then she wanted to take my pants off and I just didn't want to. . . . I'm beginning to feel like such a freak—cold, gay, whatever."

Despite the oral exam, I graduated with honors.

At the graduation ceremony, which was outdoors, a crazy woman from town named Cosmic Lady yelled from the back, "All right, all you motherfuckers and fatherfuckers!"

In the sunny courtyard I stood and smiled with my parents as an acquaintance took our photo.
Ken hadn't come up for the ceremony.

• • •

Evaluation for my fiction workshop: "His stories 'The Neptune Visitor' and 'The Mother' both tried to capture the tragedy of human alienation and the results were provocative. The language Cliff employed in most of his stories allowed for the narrative to take place on two levels, and even though this may not have been his intention, it worked well."

SUMMER 1980

I moved my stuff out of the dorm and back to my parents' house in San Jose.

At breakfast, the rubber-banded box of frozen sausages and the plastic bag of frozen diminutive corn muffins.

I rubbed our dog's floppy tan ears, which were whitish with age.

My father had retired two years earlier but my mother still worked part-time, as a bookkeeper for a cultural organization.

"He just sits in his chair all day," she whispered.

During an argument over Christmas break, she had said to me, "Why are you shutting me out?"

I continued trying to decide what to do about Liz.

I went for a run—lawn, street, lawn, street, lawn, street, and scarcely a person to be seen.

All the houses made of stucco.

I considered visiting old teachers but decided against it.

I mowed while my father carefully trimmed along the sidewalk.

I napped on my old bed, feeling the perfect breeze that always blew through that house.

A summer dinner from childhood: corn on the cob, sliced ham, sliced tomatoes, and watermelon for dessert.

"Oh, that's good!" said my father.

The jasmine blooming along the fence under the window of the dining room.

The speckled whitish slightly bumpy linoleum under my feet.

"You knocked the heating register out of place," said my father, so I bent to fix it.

My parents sat watching TV, which I disdained.

I drove my mother's white boxy Dodge to the house of an old high school friend, and we went to see *The Shining*.

"Heeeere's Johnny!"

. . .

In the darkened theater I began to shake uncontrollably.

When I got home, my parents had gone to bed and the house was dark.

"Tonight I saw the most frightening movie that I have ever seen in my life. . . . I'm very upset. I'm even crying a little because it was so upsetting. . . . I feel like I'm on LSD. . . . When I came into the house—suddenly I understood paranoia. Literally everything is potentially frightening, harmful. I just looked at the [blank] TV screen and the reflection in it and a chill went down my back. . . . Mirrors or open doorways seem horrifying—what is to be seen in them? . . . The most frightening image: a hallucination he has. God, I almost can't say it. . . . The man sees a beautiful woman get out of the bathtub. This is hurting me to talk about it. He embraces her, but when he looks in the mirror, he sees she is old, wrinkled, scabby. There. I'm through it. . . . And I'm paranoid again; my heart is beating. . . . I really feel like I'm going crazy. Or I see how people go crazy. . . .God, it is awful to see these things in yourself. . . . The world seems scabby, wrinkled. I'm afraid I'll start hallucinating. I keep telling myself that a movie can't hurt me. Actors, sets, film only. . . ."

I woke my mother and we sat up talking at the dining room table; I told her how I felt pressured to be with Liz; my mother looked uncomfortable.
Still, she was a comfort to me that night.

・ ・ ・

A few days later I returned to Santa Cruz, where I found a share in a house not far from Mike's.

"I am feeling almost normal again but I'm still a little scared; and all the pressures that led up to that night are still there."

A dream in which my parents are unkind to me: "I just remembered the end . . . I ran into my room. [My brother] Ken was there, and he was extremely understanding; his face was like a kindly Buddha or something. Of course that scares me. . . . Yet I want to think about that face of Ken's . . . a refuge from all the accusation, irritation, lack of compassion, and frustration. I'm not sure what Ken symbolized."

How at any given moment you never quite know what life you're in the midst of hatching.

Whenever I moved anywhere, I always set up my stereo first.

There might have been a confrontation with Liz, or maybe I simply hoped not to run into her in town.

The ones Kate doesn't want, the ones who dance her around.

Someday I would claim Fred's faggy voice as my own: record album as prophecy.

・ ・ ・

In listening again now, I pay homage to the sacred blind task of destroying and remaking myself.

Something sacred in records themselves—in the act of placing the disk, then the needle.

The odd miracle of the needle in the groove.

The knitting quality of any music with a beat.

The knitting quality of the crackle of vinyl.

I've always loved songs that go through phases, such as when the guitar riff changes in "Rock Lobster" and an insect begins to croak.

I was becoming in some ways exactly what I wanted to be, and in other ways, exactly what I didn't want to be.

My room was at the front of the house, and instead of coming through the front door, Mike simply climbed in my window.

I got a temporary job working graveyard shift for Intel, testing chips.

Cathy wrote suggesting I move to New York, where she was working for the Strand bookstore.

Exhausted from my shift, I walked home along the water, under the early morning clouds.

• • •

Cindy singing "rock lobster" again and again, "operatically"—child imitating a diva, or mouse singing in an old cartoon.

The year I didn't lose my virginity; the year I learned to read, that is, ironically; the year I began writing fiction; the year I traded Joni Mitchell for the B-52s; the year I met Cathy, befriended Chris and Ellie, and grew close to Mike; the year I nearly flunked; the year I lost my mind.

"But the future pops in my mind again," I wrote. "What do I want? I don't seem to know in the least."

# 12

## HOW TO BE A GIRL

Pretenders: *Pretenders* (Sire Records, 1980)

### Lisa Dierbeck

"I'm the ring leader, and they're my lions."
—Chrissie Hynde, referring to her band

### 1. THE HARBINGER

I first heard the Pretenders coming through an open window. I stood on the leafy terrace of my parents' apartment, head bowed. "It is time! For you! To *stop*," the singer proclaimed, accompanied by a nasty, nervy band. The song's impact was strikingly physical: a sensation, a blow. I was captivated by the melodic tune and the hammering beat. The lyrics were delivered with an impassioned authority that had me riveted.

The record was being played in my neighbor's house, and I couldn't make out all the words. I lingered to hear the rest of the song while watering the violet petunias in their hanging baskets. The barbarous drums entered my bloodstream and made me agitated. I longed to bolt up my fire escape and run across the rooftops towards the source of the music, whooping and screeching.

I could see Jamie-the-Guitarist, perched on his windowsill, four houses east of our building. He didn't have a shirt on. He had wrapped a sash, or maybe it was a tie, around his head. It made his hair stand on end even more than usual, accentuating the clusters of ringlets that surrounded his ashen face. He gazed in my direction from behind his tinted aviators; a half-smile played on his lips.

Jamie had sent the new Pretenders album blasting out of his huge, magnificent speakers. They loomed behind him, in the murk of his bedroom, like a pair of black Egyptian obelisks. I stole peeks at Jamie and his stereophonic kingdom while pretending to watch the neighbors' terrier chase a squirrel around a flowerbed in the formal garden below. Jamie and I were separated by a distance of fifty feet. We communicated with hand signals and sidelong glances; we rarely spoke. When the album was finished I raised my hand, forming a circle with my index finger and thumb to say, "Yeah, I like it, thank you."

Jamie-the-Guitarist ducked inside and disappeared from view. Three years earlier, he'd moved to my block with his mother, a divorced socialite. Ever since, he'd been introducing me—and all the inhabitants of the surrounding buildings—to cool music. Each new band transported me to an exotic land. Figuring out what song Jamie had transmitted through the airwaves was a challenge; I tried to identify his songs during sleepovers at friends' houses, listening to their stereos, and I searched for them on my portable transistor radio.

When he played *Pretenders*, I was in my junior year of high school. The album coincided with a turning point in my outlook—an unexpected moment of discovery.

## 2. THE TOM BOY

A tall, angular woman stands alone, one foot planted in front of the other, as if she's ready to sprint. She has a curvy, sleek electric guitar strapped over one broad shoulder, and she's slung her instrument low against her slender, boyish hips. Fingers on the frets, she aims her Fender at the camera. She might, in another time and place, be holding a machine gun, dressed in camouflage, leading a revolt. Instead, she's wearing a sleeveless black shirt that draws attention to the sinewy white bareness of her arms. Her narrow, slim-fitting trousers are adorned with leopard spots. She must have borrowed her boots from Nancy Sinatra: they're made for walking. Her kohl-rimmed eyes and dark bangs bring to mind Louise Brooks, the feline silent movie siren. Her haircut is emphatically impractical. It obscures her eyes entirely. Her bangs are too long by a full inch, a sexy blindfold, brushing the bottom edge of her lower eyelashes, disguising her identity, transforming the wearer into a woman of mystery. Hair in the eyes defies common sense and parental decree. On the night I cut my hair to emulate her, not long after hearing the Pretenders, my mother complained: "Let me trim your bangs, dear, they're impairing your vision." Evidently, Chrissie Hynde doesn't need to see. Of course not. She's a rock star, isn't she?

Stars are born. There was inevitability to her apotheosis. Yet, during the same years I spent leafing through the pages of *Tiger Beat*, the talented, ambitious Hynde was floundering. Through the 1970s, before she formed her group, she was treading water in England and America, unable to make a dent in the music industry. She became so demoralized that she was reduced to riding back and forth on the Tube alone, crying and drinking cheap wine from a bottle. She floated around for several long, fruitless years, an undiscovered rock star without a band or a record. She was not unanimously liked by the men she later assembled for the Pretenders' first recording. British musicians she collaborated with saw her as loud, vulgar, and aggressive. She impressed one colleague as "a bitch." She must have frightened those English boys, back in the mid-'70s, when the British music establishment was rife with a casual, reflexive misogyny.

Those same unquestioned principles governed my household. Girls growing up when I did existed in a man's world.

### 3. DISTURBANCE AT THE PANTHEON

It was not this exact photograph, but one very much like it, that, as a teenager, I tore out of a magazine and hung on the wall above my bed. From childhood, it had been my practice to thumb through periodicals and rip out pictures of rock stars. Using a complicated color code I'd worked out, I'd draw a thick line around a musician's silhouette—mauve crayon for Eric Clapton, lavender for Neil Young, magenta for Mick Jagger—and cut it out, like a paper doll, gluing the photo onto a thin strip of oak tag. I taped my two-dimensional puppets onto a sheet of metallic paper that covered my bedroom wall. The figurines could be attached and reattached, so the mural kept evolving.

The mural had been a pet art project for as long as I could remember. It had started when I was in nursery school with Beatles memorabilia. The first rock album my family had owned was *Sgt. Pepper's Lonely Hearts Club Band*. I can recall opening it up and marveling at the handsome faces of the four young men. They were dressed like toy soldiers, in the gold-tasseled uniforms of a fanciful marching band. The album's packaging came with paper cutouts—four illustrations of mustaches based on the ones sported by John, Paul, Ringo, and George. The mustaches could be pulled out, carefully, with an adult's help, along the perforated cardboard. As a little girl, I used to listen to the Beatles while gleefully spinning in dizzying circles, a dot of adhesive on my upper lip holding Paul McCartney's mustache in place.

I acquired other fashion accessories. I demanded a gun in 1967, when I was four, at the height of the Vietnam War. My mother, a peace activist, was horrified. After much pleading, I was given a water pistol made of fragile orange plastic. I added a holster and a helmet to my prop department, a long-handled rubber dagger to my arsenal. I'd absorbed the pop culture of the period, consuming contradictory messages that split jaggedly down the fault line at society's center: the flower children to the left of me, the macho tough guys to my right. Cops vs. robbers; cowboys vs. Indians; girls vs. boys—these were the games we played at recess in the schoolyard. I was unhealthily fascinated by "boy stuff," as my aunt had scolded. I didn't know how to be a girl.

No baby dolls for me, no tiny bottles, no frilly bonnets or pint-size diapers. I opted instead for Hot Wheels model racing cars. I liked medieval knights in armor, wielding lances and swords. I had a hundred little green army men and a boxful of molded plastic weaponry. Before I knew my Play-Doh from my Silly Putty, I'd thrown my hat in with the boys.

Even to a four-year-old, male supremacy was evident. My earliest role models had been television heroes, the dashing men of *The Wild Wild West* and *The Big Valley*, racing to and fro on horseback, a posse of clean-shaven actors in spurs, sideburns, and tight pants. The Rifleman, a sharpshooter with a Winchester and an assassin's coldhearted gleam in his eye, went on explosive killing sprees, gunning down lawbreakers. He was, of course, the good guy. And how I admired Daniel Boone, in his raccoon-skin cap, and the Lone Ranger, in his jaunty neck-scarf, studded holster, and black eye-mask, riding Silver, his galloping white stallion.

My heart's desire was unachievable: I wanted to be one of them.

I hated girls. Evidence of girls' cravenness and mediocrity was everywhere I looked. In *I Dream of Jeannie*, the voluptuous, midriff-bearing Barbara Eden was one pair of harem pants away from the centerfold of *Playboy*, a magazine the postman delivered to our door twelve times a year. Jeannie had supernatural gifts, yet was beholden to her "master"; when she spoke, she sounded like a twit. In *Bewitched*, Elizabeth Montgomery's character, Samantha, suppressed her powers so she could be a housewife. She was intelligent, yet easily intimidated by her idiot husband Darrin.

The flickering, rectangular screen of the television set reflected the mechanics of our family, the social architecture of our living room. My dad ruled. An ex-playboy, he was an award-winning filmmaker who wore a suede cowboy hat with a silk ascot tied around his throat. He roamed the globe on daring expeditions, accompanied by an all-male camera crew, traveling on desert roads in a mud-splattered jeep. My mom stayed home to cook, clean, and take care of me.

I plotted my escape from Planet Gender. While my girlfriends were baking charming little frosted cakes in their Suzy Homemaker ovens, I was in the next room with their older brothers, playing strip poker. David, Roger, Peter, Scott, Chris, Arthur, Ron, Sam, Ira, Adam, Dave, Miles, Don, Mark, Rick: boys who played music for me in their rooms. Sometimes I just lounged around in a boy's bunk bed, checking him out, inhaling his odor, listening to songs he liked, running my thumb along the spines of the albums on his shelf. Sometimes we took our clothes off, or teamed up to pilfer prescription pills from a parent's medicine chest. Every boy was my talisman, my Aladdin's lamp. If I got as close as I could, his maleness might rub off on me. Through osmosis, I'd lay claim to all my missing pieces, the strength, status, and confidence that belonged to me but that some thief had stolen.

Bob, Robbie, Robert, Jimmy, David, Mick, Keith, Ron, Charlie, Lou, Paul, John, Ringo, George, Rod, Johnny, Iggy, Peter, Gene, Steven, Alice (Cooper): boys I cut out and put up on my wall. Musicians in boys-only bands warbled to us like male songbirds in mating season, those afternoons after school, while we hung around idling and dreaming, putting off doing our homework. Their voices formed a protective force field, including me in the clique, temporarily admitting me into the men's club, embracing me in testosterone.

Some days, smoking dope, I gave the rock stars things they didn't have. I bestowed a strand of fake pearls upon Rod Stewart, hanging them from a pushpin I'd stuck into his neck. I spent hours making elaborate tableaux. I photocopied Bob Dylan, doodled on his face, folded him in half, and set him afloat inside the goldfish bowl. Dylan sank in the miniscule nation I reigned over, but John Lennon walked over water. The waves encircling him were cerulean blue, dappled by flecks of light made of glitter glue. I scribbled over Robert Plant's photograph so hard one afternoon that I tore his head off. I crucified Steven Tyler in the spring of 1980. I rebelled against my idols, defaced my gods.

I was midway through my sixteenth year of life. Now I was a girl, whether I liked it or not, but of a specific variety. I was the sort of girl who carried a black satin evening purse to high school instead of a book bag. My two best girlfriends and I shared this purse between us, taking turns holding it. A certain legal risk was involved for the carrier because our clutch was filled, in one zippered pouch, with twenty grams of loose cocaine and, in the other, three foil packets of latex condoms. Thus equipped, I set my sights on seducing my sultry, heavy-lidded neighbor, Jamie-the-Guitarist.

I would pursue him, I decided, like a huntress. Recently, I'd noticed, my flings had acquired a whiff of hostility. I didn't so much woo a guy as target him for an ambush. Like a formidable enemy, he had to be subdued with sedatives, bound at wrist and ankle, prepared for ritual slaughter. This savagery was what I heard in the Pretenders. The day I bought their first album, I holed up by my stereo and played it repeatedly. It made me so happy that I pogoed up and down and spun around like a dervish until I felt sick. I recognized it as my recording, a piercing, articulate chronicle of my exploits. These were my victory cries, my dirges.

The songs read like chapters in a novel: "The Phone Call," "The Wait," "Tattooed Love Boys," "Mystery Achievement." The album tells the tale of a lone adventuress. It's her saga, her movie, her bible.

"Gonna hurt some, child," she bluntly acknowledges on one adrenaline-charged cut. The rapid-fire shifts in mood and tempo are mirrored by her volatile voice, now wise and sympathetic, now cruel and taunting. She chants "child" at the end of each phrase, in lacerating repetition, as if marking an end of childhood, an expulsion. Words burst forth in flashes, punctuating the music like beating fists. "Hurts!" she yelps, curiously exultant, an ecstatic, all-accepting embrace of experience. She urges the listener forward, rushing open-armed towards life's beautiful and painful places, offering no salve, no protection. This is music for the daring and the fearless.

On one song, I heard my own distress signal. "Lust turns to anger, a kiss to a slug," Hynde sings, weary, lucid, shattering. She is observing without passing judgment, filing an accurate and honest report from the battlefield of sex and violence. She changes tone within seconds, quicksilver, sliding into frank eroticism. Breathy, smoky-voiced, she's suddenly a punk Mae West, hand on hip, winking, knowing, provocative, as she sings of how "the veins bulged on his . . ." And? She teasingly delays her delivery, pausing suggestively before finishing the line—"*brow.*" Before the track ends, it turns wry, sly, sensual, wounded, anguished, rapturous. It is a raucously complex love song.

I threw off my headphones to fling myself exuberantly around my bedroom. Minutes later, I punched the wall mural, poking holes in the shiny silver paper as tears streamed down my cheeks. The emotion took me off guard, shocked me. Hot-blooded, cold-hearted, I often behaved like the Rifleman, as if I didn't have any feelings.

I went back to the album again and again, trying to decipher the lyrics like runes, conjuring a new definition of the word I'd despised. Chrissie Hynde embodied a whole different way to be female. She made the sound of a chick on fire, blazing a trail.

### 4. LOLITA'S LAMENT
Girl.

I first made contact with Jamie-the-Guitarist three years before he played the Pretenders for me. I was thirteen years old. It had given me an electrifying thrill. I felt as though I'd broken into a cage at the zoo and pet the lion's nose. All I had done, though, was raise my hand one summer afternoon as I reclined on the deck chair. I waved at him. A long time seemed to pass before the figure in the window acknowledged my greeting. Then he lifted his hand and spread his fingers.

From afar, Jamie struck me as a deeply romantic figure. I'd fallen early and hard for his record collection, which seemed never-ending and up-to-date, and for his deliciously degenerate physical appearance. He was a pale, thin guy of indeterminate age with wiry, upright hair in the shape of a head of broccoli. Like Bozo the Clown, whom I'd liked as a child, Jamie had hair shaded a candied, artificial orange. That hair was luminous, a bright beacon of countercultural oddity on our Upper East Side street, with its tended window boxes of geraniums and uniformed doormen in brass buttons and epaulets who stood guard like palace sentinels. We lived along a row of stately homes off Park Avenue. Several of the residents, myself included, owned fluffy white French poodles. No one littered on those pristine streets, it seemed, and no one cursed or yelled on the staid, hushed sidewalks. Certainly, no one else played the Clash at top volume at two a.m., or blared the Stooges early on a Sunday morning. There were just two of us who loved that music, and loved to play it loud: me and Jamie.

Jamie was unpopular. He played records continually; I cranked them only once in a while, when my parents weren't around. Mr. Majumdar, who taught yoga downstairs from our apartment in his studio on the second floor, claimed Jamie played music at criminally high decibels, causing a grave disturbance of the peace. I'd seen police officers walk up to Jamie's threshold and ring the doorbell. They talked to Jamie's housekeeper, who wore a white dress and white shoes, nurse-like. While the cops were on the block, the volume would decline, but it grew audible again as soon as they had left.

Sometimes I spied on Jamie's house at night through my mom's bird-watching binoculars. I once saw him kiss a girl in his room, pulling her toward him by the hips while her bare arm reached out to close the shutters. I spent an hour or so watching him talk on the phone, twirling the cord behind him, pacing back and forth. One night, I witnessed him entering the parlor floor of his house, walking beneath a glittering chandelier, opening a cabinet, and devouring a bag of potato chips. Jamie owned an electric guitar. Some nights he folded himself up on the windowsill, knees bent, and cradled his instrument against him. I never saw him play.

I had boyfriends, but none of them were quite this fascinating. I kept track of Jamie's habits, day to day. His shutters were closed in the mornings, when I showered and dressed and left for school, but they were open when I came home in the late afternoon. I didn't often see him outside, on our street, in daylight, but I followed in his footsteps, musically, buying whatever album I thought Jamie had been playing. I'd take the money I'd earned babysitting and haunt the record shop on Lexington Avenue, impressing the unshaven clerks there with the sophisticated nature of my purchases: Roxy Music, the B-52s, the New York Dolls, Brian Eno, Television, the Sex Pistols. By the time I started high school, I had assembled a decent sampling, though it was just a pallid imitation of the comprehensive collection curated by the master connoisseur.

Aside from his musical taste, I actually knew nothing about Jamie except the tantalizing tidbits that I'd overheard once or twice while my mom talked on the telephone. Jamie, it was rumored, had been kicked out of an elite boys' boarding school. Someone said he'd been up on drug charges, narrowly escaping jail.

We were divided, like Romeo and Juliet, by prohibition. My parents, usually indulgent and strenuously liberal, had forbid me to have anything to do with him.

"Walk by him without saying a word if he ever speaks to you," my dad had commanded, reddening. "He's a creep. Don't go near him."

Who ever listens to parents? I didn't. During the

spring, summer, and fall, I lay on our terrace in a lawn chair, always aware of the young guitarist in his attic window, a shining prince held captive in a tower. He was never still when I looked over at him. His shoulders swayed from side to side and his chin bobbled up and down. He wriggled on his sill and smiled cryptically from behind the tinted aviator glasses that shielded his face like a visor. An otherworldly glow emanated from his window after dark. He wore earphones, each the size of a half-grapefruit. From my spot on the terrace, Jamie looked like a regal red-haired extraterrestrial, like David Bowie in *The Man Who Fell to Earth*, his rocket-ship set for takeoff.

I was coming home from school one afternoon when I caught sight of Jamie on the sidewalk, on the loose. He was leaning against the fence in front of his grand, gated townhouse. Near him, chrysanthemums and ivy trailed out of two giant urns, almost the same height as Jamie. He was not much taller than I was, and, it must be said, undistinguished to look at. He was a squat, unwashed young man, flabby and soft around the waist.

We nodded at each other. I slowed down, coming to a stop outside his gate.

" 'Lo," he muttered, or something to that effect. Jamie's lips were badly chapped. He gnawed at them as he stood there, grasping the iron fence a bit too tightly, as if he were inside a speeding car. An excruciating silence engulfed us before he finally spoke. "I turned you on to the Pretenders," he said somberly. "Did'ja like 'em?"

There was something off about him, I allowed myself to notice. His speech was slightly impaired. He sounded like a man I'd once met at an elderly aunt's funeral, an old guy in a wheelchair who'd just recovered from a stroke.

But what Jamie had said was true. He'd started playing the Pretenders album a few weeks earlier, and I went crazy for the band. So I thanked him. He appeared not to be listening to me, however. He was conducting an invisible orchestra, his arms waving like seaweed drifting on an ocean current. Minutes passed. I watched sympathetically, with mild embarrassment.

He blinked. "It sounds good on my new speakers," he said, conspiratorially, jerking back to attention. "Come upstairs, if you want. I'll show you. In my room."

There was nothing to hold me back. I'd gone up, often, to guys' rooms. It was the one thing I'd dedicated myself to, these urban explorations, uptown or down, East Village or Carnegie Hill, the Bronx, Brooklyn, Queens, New Jersey, Staten Island. The rooms of boys: my favorite places, safe houses, sanctuaries, temples. But I hesitated with Jamie. I, who took pride in never turning down an offer, declined.

I had already bought the Pretenders album, I said. I added, to be polite, that I'd like to come over some other time.

The door behind Jamie was open to a well-appointed foyer. Peering in as I walked past, I caught glints of polished wood and brass, subdued wallpaper in russet and green, a console table, a vase, a framed print, a coat rack.

Deeper into the house, a sweeping Cinderella staircase emerged from the elegant gloom.

I left him on the sidewalk, a very stoned fellow—let's face it, a shut-in, a junkie, gazing upward at the heavens. My own universe had expanded, just then, and it was bigger than I'd realized. I'd overturned the pantheon with scissors and tape, placing a rock goddess at the top of my pyramid, a bright hot guiding star.

# BLUES FOR A SEMESTER ABROAD

Gloria Estefan: *Mi Tierra* (Epic Records, 1993)
## Asali Solomon

In 1985, the Miami Sound Machine, led by Gloria Estefan, erupts onto the pop scene with "Conga," a watery salsa that is as catchy as it is torturous. I'm a student at a mostly white private school in the Philadelphia suburbs. I suffer through "Conga" at school dances, where I spend a lot of time in the bleachers with fellow black girls and other undesirables. "Conga" plays on the soundtrack of the worst nights of my middle school life.

The years advance, happily putting distance between me and seventh grade. Gloria lives her life and I live mine. I transfer to a public high school in the city; I'm not a social sensation, but I don't feel like a human mushroom cloud either. If I go to a party and there's a slow song, a boy might ask me to dance. Gloria and Miami Sound Machine continue to release songs that I find strangely shameful—"1-2-3," "Rhythm Is Gonna Get You"—energetic and idiotic odes to the beat. She goes solo and wears dresses on music award shows that strike me as not just ugly but confusing. I deplore her reedy voice on "Coming Out of the Dark," and her deployment of Uninspired Black Choir for Hire #2,066. America does not agree. "Coming Out of the Dark," a dramatic ballad she debuts on the American Music Awards, a kind of bargain-basement Grammys—she is *so* American Music Awards—becomes a number one hit. She is crowned the "Queen of Latin Pop" by whoever handles such coronations, and I head off to college in New York City.

In 1994, my roommate/best friend and I leave Morningside Heights (that's *Harlem,* Columbia, *Harlem)* for a junior semester abroad in the Dominican Republic. We hope to master Spanish, learn Caribbean dances, send postcards home from the warm beach in winter, and enjoy the magic of youth and travel. Best Friend is tall and blond and I am shorter, dark-skinned with naps cut close to my scalp. I can see us then, a few weeks before departure, having a conversation about how things might be difficult for her and easier for me, since I look more "Dominican" and she is clearly *gringa.* We face each other in a tiny dorm room with a dingy tile floor and painted concrete walls; she looks tentatively brave. I feel for her and am ready to be there for her, but I am also thinking: Now is my chance! At life! I am from Philadelphia and she is from San Francisco; we have only gotten far enough in New York to know that Dominicans are the black people who speak Spanish, and that they come from a poor, tiny island that they share with Haiti. We have not gotten very far.

When we step off the plane in Santo Domingo, it seems that our suspicions will be confirmed; a weak-tea-colored official in the customs booth takes one look at Best Friend, stamps her passport, and says wryly, "Too white." We laugh uneasily. Then on the bus from the airport in La Capital, a gangly black girl in braids, who has been in this program a semester already, perches nearby and monologues in a smothered, hysterical voice about the men who have grabbed her breasts on the street and thrown rocks or trash at her, and explains the meaning of *haitiana fea*—"ugly Haitian." She says I must be ready for the men who will yell out *morena*, which might only mean "brown girl," but when yelled on the street has all the charm of "horny black bitch." Occasional street-lights in the soupy darkness pass over her face at jagged intervals. The scene recalls the deep creepiness of Marlon Brando's revolving bald head in *Apocalypse Now*. I wait for her to whisper about "the horror."

Now, as I write this, I can tell you all the things that Best Friend and I don't know as we settle into Santiago. We don't know that Santiago is the whitest city in the Dominican Republic. We don't know that when we go to the beach a week into the trip, a guy selling knick-knacks will call me *nee-ger* and then a few steps away another will call me *darkie*. We don't know that these men will be dark enough to be members of my family, but for them, in this country, light enough to call me out. We don't know that hundreds of years of slavery and colonization, and the Haitian Revolution, have created a nation largely descended of African slaves who suffer from a life-shaping fear of blackness. We don't know that this fear, mixed with Caribbean inventiveness, has spawned an entire language to describe every known combination of skin color, nose width, and hair texture, and that neutral terms like "black" and "brown" are often insults. We don't know that in 1937 the Dominican dictator massacred tens of thousands of Haitians, considered a black scourge, at the border. We don't know that the current president regards the massacre as a patriotic act. We don't know that the university where we study boasts students who agree. We don't know that a mix of this seething self-hatred with hyper-machismo means that dark-skinned women are synonymous with two things in this country: fucking and ugliness.

Who can tell, when what is happening to them is not the chemistry of individual encounters, but instead the grind of history? By the time a friendly leftist professor in a late afternoon history class explains to us just about everything I have written here, it is so very late. I know it is late because she explains in Spanish and by then I've learned enough Spanish to understand everything she says. By then I've already heard *haitiana fea*, *morena*, *negra*, and *dame una bola* ("give me a ride") over and over and over again while walking the endless tropical half mile to and from school four times a day (I walked home for lunch). I've already had my name screamed nastily by my Dominican host "mother" because she confused "Asali" with the black maid's name, which was "Ysenia." I've already observed that the black maid and any black folk living here, especially women, have it inconceivably, unthinkably worse than my leaving-in-April self. I've already argued with a man on a bus who demanded that one of the other women in the group, darker than me, give up her seat to Best Friend because *morenas* are strong while white women are delicate, and watched, in a way that I will later try to forget, as Best Friend declined his help *graciously*. I've already heard the (true!) story about how two of the black students, a man and a woman, were strolling home after midnight when members of the Guardia, the paramilitary police, brandished automatic weapons and demanded that he trade her for his life, and no one was killed or raped only because they grew bored by his refusals. I've already heard the story about another Guardia, who pointed a sawed-off shotgun at one of the other black students and tried to put him on a pickup truck with a bunch of hapless dark people who may or may not have been Haitian; the doorman to his host family's building had to intervene to save him. I've already had the experience of my Dominican host family telling me, "*No hay racismo aquí.*" *There's no racism here.* By the time we understand what is happening Best Friend is zigzagging across the country with her Dominican boyfriend, his friends, and other un-black American girls on an international triple date, and I have drifted into a clique of black girls who sit in an abject clump in glittering dance clubs night after night, running out of things to say, while men trip over themselves to dance with the lumpiest pit-faced *rubias*.

Instead of succumbing immediately to the complex that this country conspires to give me, I develop a crush on one of the black American men on the trip. T—— is one of the most beautiful men I have ever been allowed to talk to. Both his eyes and arms seem to have the capacity to hold me. Even more appealing, he is weird as shit. Here is a man who is an avid fan of Sting and admits it; who carries with him a treasury of stories about cats and reads it. I know what you might be thinking and that might be true as well, but here I am a twenty-year-old virgin, weird as shit, too. Why not?

I try to keep it normal, but these are not normal days. T—— recklessly inflames my passion by laughing at my jokes, talking music with me, and complimenting my haircut. The journal that had been a faithful report of travel clichés (oh, the tasty fruits!), racial shockers, and abandonment by Best Friend, degenerates into field reports from a stakeout. I describe how close I manage to get to him in class, at the museum, in the ice cream line. I reproach myself for writing too much about him. The journal, along with letters to my therapist and friends and gazillion-dollar phone calls to my family, becomes a living shrine to T——.

Things come to a head near the end of the trip, on a boat ride off the coast of the ethereally beautiful Samaná. I "happen" to be sitting next to him, as we bob on azure waters and gaze on deep green hills in the distance, while nearby one of the other black men in the group romances a white girl.

Look at that, T—— murmurs. What do the sisters in the group think of that?

Things are loose here, I tell him. Anyway, I say, trying to be worldly, every black man has a white girl story.

I have one, he says. And he tells me the story, which sounds like blah-blah-blah because I'm too excited by the fact that we're sharing our souls and pretty soon he's going to lean into my lips and be the end of all my Dominican troubles; because it would be the last laugh on this accursed country to leave it with him; and then we disembark from the boat in the ochre glow of sunset and he runs off to make a pass at the straight-up whitest white girl available. My last dream of the trip is dead; my emotional resistance is down. Re-enter Gloria Estefan.

I hear it countless times before I *hear* it. At first all music in Spanish, from the polyrhythms of salsa to the more straightforward 2/2 of merengue and the tinny melancholy of bachata, all sounds the same to me. That is to say, like major-key parade music coming from a forgotten radio. But music plays everywhere in the Dominican Republic, even in laced-up Santiago, and so in my alienation, I begin to discriminate. First I am able to tell different songs apart, later different genres. Then I become aware of Gloria Estefan's voice. An instant later it's ubiquitous, this record, her first in Spanish. It is playing in La Crepería, where I sometimes go to drown my blues in silvery sweet piña coladas; on the black stone beach at Barahona, where over spring break I drag Best Friend away from her new boyfriend and back to me; in the *campo*, where a dirt-poor farming family treats me like a real person. Occasionally it plays in the discos, where I watch couples whirl and dip with savage precision. Finally, like a hostage who realizes she's fallen in love with one of her captors, I recognize that *Mi Tierra*, which is the embodiment of Estefan's rabid, crappy anti-Castro politics and sounds like a big corny Pan-Latin musical, has infiltrated the stereo of my soul. I am learning Spanish through learning song lyrics and learning song lyrics by learning Spanish, especially after I break down and ask a friend to make a tape of her copy for me. The creeping process of my comprehension is like seeing an image from several stingy angles and then suddenly seeing the whole thing. First I can hear the words; then I can see them spelled out in my mind. Finally I understand them enough to know the mood of the record and feel the fantasies of the songs. I love *Mi Tierra* in 1994 because I master it when I feel incapable of mastery. I love it because, like all good pop music, it is a poetic distillation for what is happening.

A little shy of the four months we had planned, I changed my ticket and flew home early. Best Friend stayed on late. After college I went to California and she moved further uptown, deeper into Dominican country. The trip is a link in the chain of our intimacy and we've talked about it endlessly and incompletely. We both wanted what young Americans want when they travel: love and adventure financed by imperial might. She was white so she got it; I was black so I didn't. I can't knock her hustle, and I will love her forever, but I have to ask: does it mean something that Best Friend never developed a taste for *Mi Tierra*?

The album often plays when I have sorted through my memories, and it exposes them as shifting and many-sided. It does this while bringing its own reality to the mix. For example, the title track is probably about rich white Cubans longing for their 1950s haciendas, but for me it was the anthem for how I never should have left Philadelphia, where only white people called you "nigger" and then it would only be an insult and not a come-on, and if you stayed within the lines that might not ever happen. But "Mi Tierra" ("My Homeland"), with its vision of exile from a *holy homeland* that *pains your soul* and *sighs when you're not there,* demands more from my imagination than hyper-segregated, dingy Philadelphia, with its dearth of palm trees and Cuban rhythms. Because, of course, the state of things in the Dominican Republic is a version of what they are in the United States, the same ingredients mixed to make a muffin rather than a cake. So "Mi Tierra" also makes me nostalgic for the homeland that I never had. The horns and drums and even Gloria's expressive wails make me *long* to long for a homeland.

In her liner notes, Estefan apologizes for the flatness of the English translations of her lyrics. "Please remember that Spanish is a very romantic language," she writes. And so the more fevered of the love songs on *Mi Tierra* were uniquely qualified to fan the flames of my obsession with T—— and score the unrequited farce that it turned out to be. But these songs, though Cuban-American Spanish and not Dominican Spanish, also mimicked the grand dimensions of the loving hatred that the Dominican Republic offered me. The intensity of lines like "Your love was the ocean that quenched my thirst" echoed the passion with which men everywhere tracked me with their eyes and loud appraisals. ("I feel like Madonna," said one of my compatriots.) The theatrical gestures of these songs were matched by a note I got at the university, passed to me by a cornmeal-colored, cologne-soaked preppie who then slipped away. One of the American students got so excited. "Is it a love note? Is it a love note?" she chirped, and it took her and several others, including my prim host mother, to translate: *Mamí, color of tobacco / All I have here is hanging for you / To love without being loved / Is like wiping yourself without shitting.* There is a depth of feeling in the person that conceived, composed, and delivered a note that said "You are shit," and the depth was in the music of *Mi Tierra*. But the music was also the medicine. Another love ballad, "Volverás" ("You'll Be Back"), partakes of a grand tradition in Spanish lyrics that revels in telling a callous lover that he (or she) will certainly be sorry, and in limning the exact shape of the coming sorriness: *You'll never erase the memories of my caresses on your skin / . . . I know you'll get tired of the deceit / And you'll be back.* When

I came back from the DR, I wanted to be my best self—to process my time there, research international racism, and keep in friendly touch with T——. But when Gloria's voice wells up in melancholy tenderness and witchy knowing over mournful Spanish guitars, I want revenge on those men, on T——, on that note writer, that country. I want them to crawl back and be sorry. And I want it now.

The song that I wish ended *Mi Tierra* but that sits in the middle instead is "No Hay Mal Que Por Bien No Venga" ("Out of All Bad Some Good Things Come"). Out of Gloria Estefan's unappealing politics and her cheesy oeuvre comes *Mi Tierra*, a record that tells me my life. Out of all bad some good comes, claim the black women I meet now and again who have studied abroad in the Dominican Republic. They say this with hollowed-out expressions covered by a smear of insane cheer. They say things like, I wouldn't trade the experience for anything. I've said this too and I'm not sure it's not a lie.

"No Hay Mal Que Por Bien No Venga" is as cool as a fat, blinking cat. It begins with a long creamy piano introduction that segues into the summary of a love affair now ended. *Our love was an ardent passion that transformed our souls*, sings Gloria, *but now is gone.* You can almost hear a shrug when she murmurs, *Perhaps it was an illusion*, and *Be happy, be happy. Goodbye.* Then the drums shift from a slow drag into a minimal rumba while Gloria repeats, almost chanting, *No hay mal que por bien no venga / No hay mal, no hay mal / No bad, no bad . . .* I don't just listen to this song; I climb inside of it, I lounge around in it and breezily address my memories. *Sure we had a few scrapes, a few laughs, danced a merengue or two, out of all bad some good things come.* Then the song ends.

# 14
# THREE WEEKS IN THE SUMMER

Joni Mitchell: *Blue* (Reprise Records, 1971)
## Colm Tóibín

It was Monday morning, August 9, 1971, and there were three weeks left of the summer before I went back to boarding school. I was sixteen. It was the town of Enniscorthy in the southeast of Ireland. Sometimes at night I wrote poetry. I played tennis in the day and hung out with my friends in the tennis club. I didn't talk to my friends about poetry. I was already skilled at keeping things that didn't match away from each other. My father was dead, but I didn't talk about that either, or indeed think about it much. My mother was working or away on holiday; I had made such a nuisance of myself on holiday with my family the previous few years that they didn't mind if I didn't come any more. I was a normal teenager—to some extent anyway—in a household where they had not come across a normal teenager before.

That Monday morning my sister or someone had bought the *Irish Times* and there was an article in it that I read with considerable interest. It was a column that appeared every week by the Northern Irish playwright Stewart Parker. The column was called "High Pop." That week's column was about a new album by Joni Mitchell. By then I already knew her song "Both Sides Now" in a version by Judy Collins and in another version, more up-tempo, which I had loved even more, by an Irish folk band called the Johnstons, whose members included Paul Brady, who went on to become one of Ireland's greatest singer-songwriters. I had seen the beautiful cover of Joni Mitchell's album *Clouds* and heard her singing some of the songs on late night radio. I had, I think, heard her sing her own version of "Both Sides Now" and been puzzled and pleased by her voice, the way she would not give into the sweetness of the melody, or the ease of the vocal line, but let something else happen, which was more difficult, more demanding, edgier.

Some of my friends had albums by Leonard Cohen, or albums that included cover versions of his songs. And other friends had albums by Dylan, such as *John Wesley Harding*, or Neil Young's *After the Gold Rush*, or Santana, or Jimi Hendrix, or the Rolling Stones. But I don't think any of them ever became obsessed with these sounds as I did with the sounds I loved. Other friends had albums by the Hollies or the Bee Gees or Elton John, which I tolerated but which didn't interest me. The only albums I had bought with my own money were *The Songs of Leonard Cohen*, every single word of which I knew by heart, and an album by the Johnstons called *Give a Damn*, which included versions of Joni Mitchell's "Both Sides Now" and "Urge for Going," and an astonishingly beautiful version of Cohen's "Hey That's No Way To Say Goodbye." (I still listen to it on CD with total pleasure.) With my birthday money the previous year I had also acquired Simon and Garfunkel's *Bridge Over Troubled Water*, and had alarmed my family deeply by listening to it over and over, day and night, until I wore it out.

And here, now, was a new album by Joni Mitchell. Stewart Parker had a great deal to say about it and every word fascinated me. His first paragraph alone was brilliant stuff:

> *Blueberries and waffles don't change their flavor, but the American Zeitgeist does: this summer I sense a mood of stasis, passivity, turning inward. Yesterday's radical oracles about the war and the credibility gap are today's commonplace facts. External reality is a con game. Attention has turned back on the self.*

I was old enough and smart enough to sense what this meant, and young enough to stare at it in sheer wonder and delight. I didn't often see things like that written down, and I was certainly not used to seeing them in the pages of the *Irish Times*—which, that very day, was also running news about a number of bloody wars, including one happening on our own little island of Ireland.

In his second paragraph Parker (whose plays I would, within a few years, come to know) wrote that Joni Mitchell was an "artist" who was "developing . . . profoundly." He mentioned that some of the songs on her new album *Blue* referred to public events ("they won't give peace a chance"), but that these references were "only brief glances away from the pursuit of happiness within the self mainly sought in a love relationship but also through the songs themselves." He wrote about the "clear, vivid imagery" of the songs and their "conversational ease." The album, he concluded, was "a gust of rain in a dry season."

I don't know how I happened to have money that morning but I did. I decided I would walk down to White's on Rafter Street in Enniscorthy, which had a room at the back where records were sold, and see if they had this new record. I explained all about it when I arrived. Yes, Joni with an "i." Yes, blue the color. The assistant said she would ask about it when the supplier next came around. But she didn't have it at the moment, she explained. I then stood for a while flicking through the stock in the back room; most of the albums were familiar to the touch, as I often came in here alone just to look at them. Then out of the side of my eye I saw the assistant opening a new box of LPs. I saw the album in her hand. Just one copy. And yes, the dark blue of the sleeve as mentioned by Stewart Parker. There in front of me, in this small town, was Joni Mitchell's *Blue*. I had the money with me and I bought it there and then and took it home.

Soon the problems began and the problems were serious. I simply could not stop listening to it. First thing in the morning, last thing at night, and all day in between. It must have been fine weather outside and the family, if they were away, must have come back. Before this, they had banned Leonard Cohen, but in a good-humored way, and not paid much attention to him. Nonetheless, I was only allowed to listen to him when there was no one around. They had barely tolerated Simon and Garfunkel. They had paid no attention to the Johnstons as long as it was turned down or I carried the record player into the other room. But this Joni Mitchell disturbed them, my mother, my aunt, friends of my mother's, and, in a vaguer way, the rest of the family too. This woman was out of her mind, they seemed to feel, not in the doleful, tuneless, and mysterious way of Leonard Cohen, but in a way that was noisy and shrill and somehow too direct and disturbing for comfort.

It made a difference to me that the *Irish Times* had called her an artist, but not to them. And maybe if they had liked her and we had made the album into a sort of free-for-all family entertainment and sung along with bits of it, I would not have become as possessive and obsessive about it as I did.

I played it for a few friends and they could see no sense in it either. One of them, the smartest, said that he liked the long and moody piano intro to the title track and nothing else. He was no use. No one was any use. It seems odd now that it was only three weeks between buying the album and going back to boarding school because it felt like a much longer time that I lived with those songs as though they were about me just as much as they were about the woman who wrote them and sang them. Or about whom I would, I desperately hoped, become.

Later, years later, when I did therapy, I was put into a trance by a psychiatrist, using heavy breathing in a controlled environment. In this new world, I suddenly could not control my grief; it all focused on one event— the death of my father. But there was also a sense that keeping back the emotion surrounding his death, holding it in all the years, repressing it, had taught me how to hold everything else in too; and this became a useful and damaging way of managing emotion.

Another time I was given the drug ketamine under medical supervision. The trance this time was one of pure and unmitigated joy. I imagined colors and saw paintings in the sky and smiled and laughed and believed the world was a wonderful place made for my pleasure.

In those sessions of therapy I learned that I lived at two ends of a scale—one made up of managed grief and pain, and the other of pure readiness to take pleasure from things, from colors, from words, from chords. It was the in-between parts that I had trouble with.

Listening now to the opening sounds of *Blue*, I find myself smiling. This is odd because, in my memory,

*Blue* is an album all about loss, the space between the "tombs in your eyes" and "the songs you punched are dreaming" that is dramatized in "The Last Time I Saw Richard." Now, as I listen to "California," I realize that I am being held by certain chords that suggest a sort of carelessness, a longing for something golden which plays against the melancholy; it lifts into the bitter, lovely plea, which I felt, even without the experience that gave rise to it, in Enniscorthy in 1971: "Will you take me as I am / Strung out on another man / California, I'm coming home."

Checking back, I realize that I must each time have put the album on the wrong way around—side two first, beginning with "California," so that for me it ended with the song "Blue." Or maybe I just played it either way and it ended that way in my memory. It doesn't matter maybe. What matters is how much I loved the experiences described in these songs, full of lost love, willful wanderings, moments of bliss and hope against bitter regret for pure romantic experiences which had taken place in deep intimacy. I loved the sheer glamour of the wanderings and longings described and then the piercing pain that came with them. I wanted to live like that and instead I was going back to boarding school.

But in my head I loved lines like "Up there's a heaven, down there's a town," which were so clever and sharp, in "This Flight Tonight." And also the sheer entry in that song into the world of pure intimacy, which I longed to have, in which you could hope too that they had "finally fixed your automobile" and that things would be "better when we meet again." I thought I knew what Joni Mitchell meant, even though I had never met anyone in the first place, and I had never even been on an airplane, and knew no one, other than our neighbors, who owned an automobile.

And when it came to the next track, "River," I was again sure I knew what she felt. There was a river in our town as well, and a main road out of the town. I had got out a few times and liked the look of things in the city. Joni Mitchell's music, her voice so filled with the smoke of experience and vulnerability and need, was a way to have for myself a world elsewhere, planning my life in that world quietly, keeping the dullness of things at bay. (Stewart Parker, by the way, thought "River" had "a maudlin tone"—yet "even it is worth listening to.")

I know that I did not understand "A Case of You." I often in those years missed the point of things. It didn't strike me for a second that she was singing about drinking an actual case of someone, as in a case of wine (even though I notice now that the words are perfectly clear), and then remaining totally sober—it dawned on me much later. I don't know what I thought she was trying to say. It was her tone that hit me. But there were moments in that soaring and beautiful song that were astonishing. There was the casual, resigned sadness of its opening line, "Just before our love got lost." And there was the dark, personal memory of "I remember that time you told me"—Joni Mitchell's voice almost whispering now, close to tears—"You said 'love is touching souls,'" and then the lift into "Surely you touched mine / 'Cause part of you pours out of me in these lines from time to time." This, as far as I was concerned, was poetry.

It was hard to imagine—indeed it still is—that all around me in our semi-detached houses was love, or something that had once been love and was still like love in some way or other. Love in 1971 for me was not when the neighbor and his wife tended the garden together, or when my mother made supper, it was when the needle touched the vinyl. On *Blue*, love was over, love was remembered in honest, sharp detail, love was impossible, love was so bitter and so sweet. And domesticity was denounced by Joni Mitchell with wonderful wit, as Richard, once so romantic and so wounded, "got married to a figure skater / And he bought her a dishwasher and a coffee percolator / And he drinks at home now most nights with the TV on / And all the house lights left up bright."

I knew whose side I was on as they screamed at me in Enniscorthy to turn that dreadful woman down. I was "gonna blow this damn candle out / I don't want nobody comin' over to my table / I got nothing to talk to anybody about."

And then there was the pain of wanting, the relentless self-revelation and self-exposure which would mean so much to me within a year or two when I found them again in the poetry of Sylvia Plath and the singing of Kathleen Ferrier, and later in the prose of Joan Didion and Elizabeth Hardwick, and later still in the poems of Ruth Padel and Louise Glück and the singing of Lorraine Hunt Lieberson. In the songs on *Blue*, even in ones as simple in their desires as "All I Want" or "Carey," or "My Old Man," which I never fully warmed to, there was something direct and deeply earnest in the description of need and loss and desire, emotions which Leonard Cohen would describe in terms less open and less vulnerable, with lots of mystery and metaphor and wit and even, God save us, irony.

I wonder if my addiction to *Blue* was about being gay in a small town and finding in those melodies and chords and those words something about the idea of being not quite right (her voice, my family said, was not quite right) that I found nowhere else. I found it in Hemingway soon and in Kafka too, but I never found it in songs from Hollywood musicals, as other gay men of my generation did, or in more obvious camp (unless Joni Mitchell at her Joniest was, in fact, the most obvious camp available at the time).

I don't think there is anything camp about the song "Little Green." Like the rest of the world, I learned later that it was a piece of veiled autobiography. It was really about Joni Mitchell having a baby when she was young and giving it up for adoption and never telling her family. But even without this knowledge there was, when you listened, a gravity about it, a tenderness, a sense of something seriously felt, emotion held in check rather than exaggerated. Joni could exaggerate when she was at her worst and her best—for example, when she sings out "O Canada!" in "A Case or You," or when she drops her voice on "blow this damn candle out" in "The Last Time I Saw Richard." "Little Green" was Joni Mitchell in some middle, mellow register of sad emotion, and when you read the words now ("Child with a child pretending / Weary of lies you are sending home / So you sign all the papers in the family name / You're sad and you're sorry but you're not ashamed") you realize how much it must have meant to write it and record it and sing it live on stage.

It matters to me still that Joni Mitchell meant business when she wrote most of these songs, that she was not laughing up her sleeve as she sang them at the effect they might have on a confused boy in a small town. It seems important that they mattered to her as much as they mattered to me.

And then there is "Blue," the song itself, with the long piano intro that my friend liked so much. It was the song I found most difficult in the beginning but, as with "A Case of You," most interesting in the end, even though I thought then (and later, for a while) that grass was what cows ate and an ass was the animal that Jesus used for transport when he went toward Jerusalem. "Blue" played with irony, even if it didn't go there fully, and the woman who wrote it had stopped feeling sorry for herself, even if just briefly. Joni Mitchell here was clever, almost resigned, almost funny, but she held on to that melancholy tone of hers. When she sang, "Hey Blue, there is a song for you," the listener had the right to feel that Blue was the luckiest guy in the world, to have this great, sad diva suddenly getting wise on his watch.

There were no record players in boarding school,

just some priests and three hundred other boys and a lot of lessons, broken by bad meals and much religious practice. I wrote my poems in peace in the study hall in the autumn of 1971 and I dreamed about the world. It was the age before the iPod or the portable CD player or decent earphones, and it is hard to imagine now. But in those three weeks at the end of the summer, the last three weeks of August 1971, this Canadian woman had transformed me and given me ideas, woken me up, put some more substance into my sadness. Her voice had filled my days with pleasure, too, and added some further iron to my soul, in case I needed it.

# 15

# NORTHERN EXPOSURE

ABBA: *Super Trouper* (Polygram Records, 1980)
Pankaj Mishra

In 1982, at the age of twelve, I bought my first music cassette from a kiosk in a small Indian bazaar. It was a pirated copy of ABBA's *Super Trouper*. There were, I remember, scratches on the cheap plastic cover, diminishing somewhat the glow of the white-clothed foursome standing under a broad arc light. As happened with almost all pirated cassettes I bought, the tape would soon tie itself in knots and would have to be thrown away. But I remember walking away with my purchase overcome with the adolescent thrill of doing something new and tantalizing.

Looking back, I realize that I hadn't heard a single line of ABBA before buying *Super Trouper*. I don't recall them being played on the only radio program devoted to Western pop music on All India Radio (AIR), which endlessly looped mainstream British or Commonwealth bands and singers from the 1950s, perhaps because it had no foreign exchange with which to pay for ABBA's catalog.

In the dark, dusty kiosk where I bought *Super Trouper*, the small picture of ABBA on the cassette glittered with all their exotic blondness, easily overshadowing the epicene Canadian Anne Murray and the blandly boyish Cliff Richard. The names themselves, when euphoniously coupled—Björn and Agnetha, Benny and Anni-Frid—spoke of the purest romance (I even knew how to pronounce Björn, thanks to the Swedish tennis champion who ruled Wimbledon in the '70s). On the other hand, their surnames—Lyngstad, Fältskog, Andersson, Ulvaeus—seemed forbiddingly foreign.

Anyway, this didn't matter to me or to my mates at school who keenly circulated among themselves whatever few, inscrutable totems of the modern world they could acquire. For much of my childhood I had lived with the suspicion that life was elsewhere, far away from our straggly settlements clinging to railway tracks, where the only source of excitement was the arrival of the express trains from big cities, when the only bookshop for hundreds of miles opened for only a few minutes of business each day. Listening to Western pop music, as much as reading *Dennis the Menace* comics and hoarding foreign postal stamps, was part of our uncoordinated lunge toward a glamorous modernity. I remember playing "Lay All Your Love on Me," song number four on side B of *Super Trouper*, for some friends: how the prefatory synthesizers immediately imposed a reverential hush, probably comparable in their drama and intensity with the effect the four opening bars of Beethoven's Fifth had on listeners in nineteenth-century Europe.

We could discriminate between performers of Hindi film music and the then-nascent pop culture that did not depend on Bombay films. But we did not develop anything like an individual taste in foreign music or books, largely due to the general climate of cultural deprivation and political conformity. In the early '80s India still paid perfunctory tribute to its founding ideals of socialism and nonalignment. Like many postcolonial countries, we'd even had a spell of authoritarian rule in the mid-'70s. Our "Great Leader" was Mrs. Indira Gandhi, hysterically warning us against the "foreign hand" (usually the CIA) that was apparently hell-bent on undermining India. All around us—in the stern slogans for family planning ("Two of Us, Two We Have") daubed on buildings, Mrs. Gandhi's political promises (bread, clothes, and housing), and the AIR-amplified harangues against the "foreign hand"—were reminders of the righteousness and the fundamental humorlessness and philistinism of a political elite claiming to build an independent postcolonial nation.

Mrs. Gandhi's government discouraged imports in order to create a self-sufficient economy; and, as in the former Soviet Union and other socialist countries, electronic items already rusting in American and European junkyards became much cherished. Luckily, a trade in pirated cassettes and smuggled tape recorders emerged just in time to gratify our quietly desperate acquisitiveness. My family had obtained its first tape recorder not long before I bought *Super Trouper*. I wouldn't have heard of ABBA had it not been for the king of the pirates (and nemesis of HMV and Polydor), a former fruit juice vendor named Gulshan Kumar who ran a bootlegging operation called T-Series. In the early '80s, he was at the beginning of a successful criminal career—which was neatly rounded off by his assassination by the mafia in 1997—and his taste in Western pop music ran no farther than the British *Top of the Pops* chart.

This explains why, growing up in small-town India in the 1970s and '80s, I missed many crucial moments in the evolution of Western popular music and knew next to nothing about its internal hierarchies: why, for instance, there was much to choose between Elvis Presley and Tom Jones, or why the Beatles should be considered superior to Boney M, an estimable disco band that became immensely popular throughout the Third World. There was more choice in the metropolitan cities, where the sons and daughters of the genteel bourgeoisie revered Bob Dylan and, indeed, could afford to buy his albums. We lived in relative darkness in our small towns. Boosted by T-Series, stalwarts of easy listening such as Cliff Richard and Engelbert Humperdinck and Paul Anka hulked across our shrunken musical landscape.

In any case, I would have had trouble following, for instance, the later works of the Beatles, which require at least a modest acquaintance with their times and preoccupations. Our grasp of English was shaky; strong British or American accents were hard work. Here, ABBA, themselves transplanted into English, was effortlessly accessible. They spoke an unaccented English and, though occasionally ambitious (the word "incomprehensible" in "Lay All Your Love on Me" must be the longest ever heard in pop music), wrote lyrics of almost overweening simplicity ("Smiling, having fun / Feeling like a number one")—perhaps why they were especially popular in former colonies whose aspirant consumer cultures were parasitic upon the European metropolis, such as South Africa, Canada, and Australia (which gave us *Muriel's Wedding*, the ultimate ABBA cult movie, and where *The Best of ABBA* remains one of the biggest selling albums).

Unknown to me—and the song "On and On and On" could give a contrary impression—ABBA in 1982 was about to break up. Married with improbable primness throughout a wild era, Ulvaeus and Fältskog had separated in 1979; Benny and Anni-Frid divorced in 1981. The accusatory strains of "The Winner Takes It All" ("But tell me does she kiss / Like I used to kiss you?") hinted at some late toe-dipping in the licentious '70s, with all the attendant regret and bitterness ("The judges will decide / The likes of me abide").

ABBA, the creators of such exuberances as "Mamma Mia" and "Money, Money, Money," could expand its emotional range only up to a point. While "Lay All Your Love on Me," with its descending chorales and synthesized harmonies, is a song so indisputably superior that even U2 felt compelled to cover it, a later song, "One of Us," which is apparently about a woman failing to revive a dead relationship, sounds much better in the parody that the BBC comedy show *Not the Nine O'Clock News* improvised: "One of us is ugly, one of us is cute / One of us you'd like to see in her birthday suit / Two of us write music, two have way a song/ Sorry, in translation, that line come out wrong."

It was always likely to happen, and a trip to Bombay in the late '80s finally broke ABBA's spell on me. There at Rhythm House, a famous record shop in the city's downtown, I discovered the Beatles in a listening booth. Busily churning out Boney M and ABBA bootlegs for the small town market, T-Series had yet to wake up to the importance of Bob Dylan; but I had friends and cousins in the metropolitan cities to make me tapes.

Shortly after I first traveled to London from India in the mid-'90s, I heard of a club entirely devoted to ABBA songs. One evening I tried to persuade my then-companion, a cultivated European, to accompany me to it. She looked a bit puzzled. Not long afterward, we went our separate ways. There was no connection between the breakup and my desire for the songs that had enlivened my drab teenage years in India—or so I would like to think. Nonetheless, I received my first lesson in just how ABBA had been tainted irrevocably by, among other things, their bad hairdos and shiny flared pants.

The golden Swedes had flourished in the 1970s, in the wake of the counterculture, offering light relief from its endless self-regard; and though I know how to speak of them in a way that invites smiles and, occasionally, a giggle of ironic complicity, I remember my first encounter with *Super Trouper* with the purest affection today.

Listening to the album again after two decades, the title song and "The Winner Takes It All" retain their emollient charm but only "Lay All Your Love on Me" emerges triumphant from the general debris of side B. This is, however, the perspective of a more cynical age. The truth is that ABBA still gives ample pleasure during bouts of drunken karaoke. Shouting along with "The Winner Takes It All," I remember my twelve-year-old self in a backwater town, and feel a twinge of gratitude for the Scandinavians who expanded, briefly but exhilaratingly, our very limited possibilities of fun.

# A RODEO GIRL ON BROADWAY

Rickie Lee Jones, *Flying Cowboys* (Geffen Records, 1989)
## Kate Christensen

In August 1989, when I was twenty-seven and fresh out of graduate school, I came to New York City, fulfilling a plan I had cherished ever since I was a bookish, violin-playing kid feeling totally out of place in the Arizona desert. I moved into a room in an apartment rented by two college friends in Brooklyn, on St. Mark's Place between Third and Fourth Avenues, where we listened to crack-war gunfire and even had a few bullet holes in our windows.

That fall, I got a job as an editorial assistant at William Morrow on Twenty-eighth and Madison. I had about an hour-long subway commute each morning, when I took the 4 or the 5 train from the Atlantic Avenue station. Sometimes my boss, a tiny, brilliant, doe-eyed editor named Susan, asked me to stay late, which I loathed having to do because my job paid peanuts with no overtime. But most evenings, at five o'clock sharp, I took the elevator down to the street with Jared, who sat at the desk next to mine and worked for Doug, the editor whose office was next door to Susan's. Down on the street, we said goodnight to each other and went off in our separate directions. Jared headed straight for the subway and I, because I needed exercise and couldn't afford a gym membership, walked all the way down Broadway, the spine of Manhattan, to catch the subway to Brooklyn from South Ferry, the tip of the island.

After Jared had gone his way, I put on my Walkman, pressed play, and flooded my head with music, my own personal soundtrack to my nightly walk through Madison Square Park, the carpet district, Union Square, the East Village, and Soho, then across Canal Street to the windy, empty, trash-blown stretches of Tribeca, and finally the deserted, tiny, crooked streets of the financial district, with its looming skyscrapers overhead, all the way down to New York Harbor. I loved this time of day. Leaving work meant shucking off my office persona and returning to my real way of being, my daydreamy, solitary, observant, arrogant, rebellious self. It was a glittering, fascinating, dramatic walk, and I never got tired of it. It was all new to me, this city, this life I had chosen for myself and embarked upon. I had no history here yet; it was all mine for the making. I was thin as a rail then, aerodynamic and streamlined; I knifed along the sidewalk, impatiently skirting slower walkers and darting madly through traffic, away from my work life and toward whatever adventures lay ahead that night.

This was by no means my first job; I'd been working nonstop since my seventh grade paper route, and I'd been supporting myself in one way or another since my junior year in high school, when I had left Arizona for the East Coast Waldorf school, where I had a full scholarship, and had worked as a babysitter and housekeeper for one of my teachers in exchange for room and board. But somehow working at William Morrow felt like my first real job, maybe because I had a salary and benefits, a nine-to-five, five-days-a-week schedule. As work went, it was fairly easy and low stress; Susan was an undemanding, generous, sympathetic boss, which was a lucky thing for me, because, to put it mildly, I was a lackluster editorial assistant, which is to say, my heart was not in it, and therefore I sucked at it. My only real usefulness to Susan was that I had a great knack for quickly reading and articulately rejecting manuscripts. Her office was piled high with boxes and boxes of these labored-over, treasured, sweat-stained, would-be books; I saw it as my Sisyphusian mission to empty these boxes, but of course they refilled as quickly as I could empty them. They kept coming, arriving every day from the various agents Susan had lunch with.

Susan seemed to have a great life, a career it might have done me well to aspire to if I hadn't had other, more egotistical and less practical ideas. She arrived at ten or so every morning on the train from Larchmont, made some phone calls and then, at noon, blew glamorously out of the office in her fur coat to lunches in restaurants I had only read about in magazines. She was usually out until three, leaving me to spend the bulk of my day answering her calls and shooting rubber bands at Jared and writing manuscript rejections and talking on the phone to the guy I was sort of dating. He would turn out to be my boyfriend for the next five years, but I didn't know that yet; I thought he was a temporary diversion, a drinking buddy. In my mind, I was single and free. I stayed out every night till almost dawn, at parties or in bars, drinking as I had never drunk before.

Consequently, I muddled my way through my workdays in a hungover, restless, time-wasting haze. It didn't matter to me whether or not I succeeded as an editorial assistant. I was just biding my time here; I had no ambition whatsoever to be a version of Susan, to sit at a desk into the evenings over a manuscript, chain-smoking, with a pile of Post-Its and a blue pencil; to have lunch with agents and writers; to go to meetings and book conferences. No, I was a writer, I was going to make it as a novelist, as soon as I really started to write, as soon as I shook the earnest dust of the MFA program out of my hair and "found my voice," as everyone at the Iowa Writers' Workshop had been so fond of saying. My interest in William Morrow was largely curious, acquisitive, espionage-like. I hotly envied all the writers whose manuscripts we published. Working at a publishing house felt like being a scullery maid in a home I someday hoped to own. I looked at those towering piles of manuscripts in Susan's office and thought,

*I'll be better than all of them.* If I had known then that my first novel would not be published for ten years, I might have slit my wrists. My dreams of writerly glory were paramount.

My friend Jared, on the other hand, was everything I was not: an exemplary assistant, a real editor-to-be, or so it seemed to me. He understood about publicity and marketing and how to calculate projected sales. He wrote fantastic jacket copy; Doug had even given him his own book to edit. He got to sit in on meetings with writers. Doug fully trusted Jared to run their little operation when he was out of town or out sick. But Jared wasn't an apple-polisher; he was wry, self-deprecating, and hilarious. Whenever the pint-sized, arrogant editor in chief strutted by, loudly name-dropping, hocking up loogies, and ignoring us peons, Jared would look over at me straight-faced in mock-befuddled, wide-eyed, goofy disbelief. When Doug and Susan were out somewhere, at lunch or at a sales meeting, Jared and I dropped all pretense of work and turned our chairs to face each other to yak about what we'd done the night before, what we were going to do tonight.

One morning, Jared came in with a tape he'd made for me. "You have to hear this," he said. "It's the new Rickie Lee Jones. You're going to love it." He handed me *Flying Cowboys.*

That night before my walk to South Ferry, I put the tape into my Walkman. I listened to it on my walk home the next night, and the night after that. In fact, every night for the next three or four or maybe even five months, *Flying Cowboys* was the primary, superlative, essential soundtrack to my walk down the island. I couldn't understand the lyrics except for snatches of breezy, cheerful lines here and there: "If you fall I'll pick you up," and "In the ghetto of my mind," and "Like a Cadillac painted by a rodeo girl." The lyrics of all the other albums I've been obsessed with and listened to over and over at various times in my life—*Tapestry*, for instance, or *Remain in Light* or *Graceland*—became over time as familiar to me as if I had written them myself; I internalized the words, made them a part of my brain structure. Carole King always seemed like another version of me—passionate, brainy, a little dorky, and earnest; likewise Paul Simon and David Byrne. They were my own people, and I sang along with them as if I had every right to appropriate their words for my own use and meld them with my own psyche.

But *Flying Cowboys* was mysterious and beyond my reach. Rickie Lee's adenoidal, high, lilting voice slurred her words as if they were throwaway, as if they were spontaneous and incidental. She sounded like the coolest girl who'd ever lived, iconoclastic, lighthearted, warm, reckless, and buoyant, the kind of friend you'd go on a road trip with, some protracted, unforgettable adventure involving cowboy boots, peyote, playing the slots in Las Vegas, eating fried eggs at a truck stop in Wyoming, sleeping under the stars in a canyon. . . . But the point was that even if I went on that exact road trip with *Flying Cowboys* playing on the car tape deck every mile of the way, I would never be as cool as she was, and I didn't even think about trying. I let her voice fill my head with the unattainable sound of someone who knew exactly how to live her own damned life at a time when I was striving to figure out how to live mine. The lyrics were obviously private, hers and hers alone to know and understand, so I didn't waste any energy trying to figure them out. Walking along Broadway day after day, I tried to make a mark of some kind, wear my own physical groove, while *Flying Cowboys* made a parallel groove in my head of jazzy, ethereal, hopeful noise. But when I got onto the train at South Ferry and turned off my Walkman—the train was lurching and loud; I didn't bother trying to listen to music as we rocketed under the river to Brooklyn—both avenue and album closed themselves to me like something disappearing underwater, slipping back into themselves, untouched by me and not mine to keep. The album resisted internalizing, remained apart from me, exactly like Broadway.

At home, I was as bumbling and embryonic as I was at work. The apartment where I lived then was a long, spacious place with a kitchen and sitting room at one end and a large living room at the other, and three bedrooms along a very long hallway. As the newcomer, I got the bedroom in the middle, which had no windows, but it did have an electric ceiling fan, and it was absolutely quiet in there at night, sheltered from all the street noise, the salsa music blaring from cars, the yelling and gunfire. I furnished my bedroom piecemeal, mostly with crap I dragged in off the street: milk crates, a futon frame, an old bureau. I didn't care that it was a dark little hole: it was mine, and I was safe there.

The former college friends I lived with were two women named Sam and Anne. I had barely known them in school, but they had now become the lifelines to my social world. They had been in New York much longer than I had; Sam was a painter who worked as an assistant to other, more famous painters, Anne was a copy editor at *Spy*. They had boyfriends, sort of, or girlfriends, sort of. Sam and Anne knew where to buy shoes and where to get the best *pho* and how to talk to the guys who sat outside the corner bodega playing cards. Anne was elegant, chic, and understated; Sam was wild and urchinlike. They both had short blond hair; Anne's haircut was a fetching sort of new wave pixie 'do, Sam's self-inflicted with nail scissors and sometimes dyed neon green or orange. Anne invited me to snarky writers' shindigs; Sam took me to wild downtown loft parties.

Like Rickie Lee, they struck me as knowing and arrived in a way I was not. I tagged along with them and watched what they did, squirreling it all away into the storehouse of knowledge I was amassing. From Anne I learned coy archness and how to work a dimple; from Sam, tough moxie, not giving a fuck what other people thought. Anne bought a rug from ABC Carpet for her sitting room; I promptly spilled beer on it. Sam and I stayed up all night smoking and drinking; I still have journal entries stained with vodka, illegible, describing what it felt like to be totally shit-faced. They are unintentionally hilarious. I was so transparently hungry for experience, extremes, Life with a capital L. And I was young enough to think other people were the answer, that I couldn't find what I was looking for unless I opened myself to people who knew more than I did and allowed them to define and impress and influence me. "You know that I love you," Rickie Lee sings in one song on *Flying Cowboys*, and it echoed for me the ease and relaxedness of her diction, her assumption of her right to say something so brazenly untormented.

My love life, at the time, was a bit of a shambles. I was sort of dating that guy, the one I'd be with for five years, although it all felt very provisional and temporary the entire time. When we met, he happened to live with his ex-girlfriend, although sometimes I wasn't so sure about the "ex" part, because she wasn't supposed to know about me. And I was still heartbroken over my grad-school boyfriend, a writer I was grossly incompatible with in just about every way except sexually but had been teeth-grittingly determined the entire final semester at Iowa to love and be loved by, as if this were some life-or-death challenge. I had, thank God, failed at this, and had thereby escaped that maelstrom. And now I was safe; I was in New York, and he was still in Iowa. But I was still horribly brokenhearted over the whole thing. "Don't let the sun catch you crying," Rickie Lee sang, and it was comforting. It's such a tender song, so matter-of-factly optimistic, and it gave me the where-withal to imagine I was over the whole affair even when I wasn't, or at least to look forward to a time when I would be, and to realize that that time really would come. The song was like a cast or a splint shoring up a torn muscle or a broken bone while it heals, or braces on teeth that are growing in wrong. *Flying Cowboys* was my false courage, my training wheels, while I figured shit out.

Now it's nineteen years later. I'm no longer in touch with Sam and Anne and Jared and Susan; I've also lost contact with both of the boyfriends I was so hung up on back then. By no means have I figured everything out, but I have in some measure achieved what I came to New York hoping to do. I've been married for twelve years, I own a house in Brooklyn, I recently finished my fifth novel, and I don't hang out in bars much anymore. I guess this is midlife.

Listening to *Flying Cowboys* today, I'm struck by the fact that I can understand the lyrics perfectly now. It could be that, for the first time, I'm listening to the album inside, on a regular CD player, without ambient noise, honking horns, trucks roaring by on Broadway. Or maybe, like a Zen koan, I can grasp them now that I've stopped trying to grab them, and they're clear as could be, and they don't seem unattainable anymore. Rickie Lee sounds so young to me now. I feel toward her a kind of admiring protectiveness. I find myself thinking, as I listen with almost motherly empathy, that I hope she never lost that breezy passion, that cool openness.

I've never listened to *Flying Cowboys* with another person. It has always been and remains a solitary album for me, not a social one. It has always transported me, like a flying carpet. First, in the old days, it carried me ahead to some imaginary, hoped-for, satisfying future. Now that that future is here, it takes me back to those days when I listened so hungrily to the voices of people who showed me the way.

# 17
## NO MOD CONS

The Who: *Quadrophenia* (MCA Records, 1973)
## James Wood

I was looking down at an incurably English breakfast plate. A greasy fried egg had been punctured, and the sluggish fluid of its heart had stained the other food: some baked beans, half of them mashed; fat, scattered chips, as thick as a man's fingers, smeared with sauce; two sausages that had been prospected in, cut open, and half-eaten; a folded slice of bread, white as paper. Around the plate were a box of matches (the old "Ship" logo was visible), a metal ashtray with two fag ends in it, salt and pepper cellars, a large glass jar of sugar, and a cup of what looked like cold tea. A fork, plunged into the pulp, and a knife on the right of the plate, with two beans glued to the blade, suggested that I had already made some headway.

It was a photograph, and I first saw it in 1978, when I was thirteen. My brother, five years older than me, and then the magical conduit for rock music, was showing me the Who's double album *Quadrophenia*, which came with a book of thirty black-and-white photographs remarkable for their grainy bleakness. *Quadrophenia*, first released in 1973, was a "concept album," which makes it sound much more pretentious than it is. Sometimes, concept albums were pretentious. Pink Floyd's *Wish You Were Here* is often opaque, and I could never make any sense of the man on the cover of that record who was dressed in a suit and apparently on fire. But Pete Townshend's concept was simple: he just wanted to tell a story—to use the album to look back at the early 1960s from the early 1970s, and to evoke the life of a typical "mod kid" of that era and the stages of his rebellion.

The book of photographs begins with a shot of a young man, seventeen or so, riding in London on his scooter. To the thirteen-year-old, this boy on a bike seemed thrillingly alone, aimlessly purposeful. And he had the full mod package. He is dressed in his army surplus parka; his scooter (probably a Vespa GS 160) bristles with extra headlights and spindly wing-mirrors. His dark hair is carefully short. In another photograph, he is seen at home, arguing with his stern middle-aged parents (his mother dressed in a towel-cloth bathrobe, and eerily resembling the Queen), looking as if he has to get out of the tiny kitchen or die. The picture of his breakfast comes next—the sick egg and beans. I stared and stared at that photo, feeling at once vaguely hungry and vaguely nauseated. We see this mod kid in a coffee bar, playing pinball; then working as a dustman, hauling a corrugated metal bin on his shoulder; then smashing up a car on the street; then watching from the roadside as the members of the Who come out of the Odeon, after a concert. After that comes a journey to Brighton—he is seen inside a café whose windows promise fish and chips, oysters, and "jellied eels." In Brighton, he runs into a friend who is now employed as a hotel bellboy, with proper uniform: his little round flat hat looks like a child's drum. But, as I could tell from the photographs, things seem to go badly for him in Brighton. He no longer has his scooter, which he smashed in an accident; he has lost his job, and is sleeping on the beach. In the last frames, he has stolen a boat and is heading out to sea . . .

*Quadrophenia* was immediately alluring as a narrative, before I had heard a minute's music. The title was strange and edgy, somehow combining "schizophrenia" with "quadraphonic"—the latter all the rage, then—as if music could be a kind of vivid sickness. Then my brother dropped the clumsy needle onto the vinyl, and the huge, customized Goodman loudspeaker he had wired up to the old Leak valve amp exploded—exploded with music. And nothing has changed in thirty years. The sound comes thinned and compressed through its digital codes, the amplifier is cleansed of its noisy, tardy valves, but the music still has tremendous power. The Who playing at full throttle is, for me, one of the indices of life. Or perhaps I should say that hearing the Who is both a way of registering life and a way of shaking a fist at it. Pete Townshend's angry, metallic guitar chords seem to slice into the softness and hypocrisy we wad ourselves with; John Entwistle's extraordinarily mobile, perpetually restless bass playing seems like the steps of a man who is running away from something (even though he was famous for staying perfectly still when playing live, while the band erupted into gymnastics around him); Keith Moon's wildly exciting drumming, both precise and slightly drunken, seems like a form of dedicated vandalism, a desire to play the drums and smash them up at the same time; and Roger Daltrey's singing is often barely indistinguishable from shouting. That to me is what rock should sound like: a concentrated, furious laboratory of focused energy.

But this is not the repetitive, mindless restlessness of heavy metal or punk (though the Who certainly influenced good punk-ish bands like the Jam and the Clash). A great deal of rock music is rhythmically dull. The guitars pound away, and the drummer just lends a solid hand. The Who is always rhythmically exciting. Moon is never exactly where you expect him to be with a roll or fill or cymbal, and finds it difficult to keep the beat for more than a bar or two before tearing off again in search of new patterns; Entwistle, always listening to what Moon is doing, dances up and down the scales; Townshend is as nimble an acoustic player as he is savage an electric guitarist. Among the greatest performers in the history of rock, they play like jazz musicians, and one of the chief pleasures of *Quadrophenia*—the quality that elevates it above *Who's Next*, the band's other great album—is its atmosphere of improvisation. In song after song, the group is listening to itself, and feeding on its own creative borderlessness.

A typical song on *Quadrophenia*, like "Sea and Sand," or "Drowned," or "I'm One," starts with a gentle, fingerpicking introduction on acoustic guitar. Daltrey is almost crooning. Then the drums and bass come in and everything is changed. Folk has surrendered to rock. Suddenly, the acoustic has been silenced by the hard flourishes of Townshend's Gibson, and Daltrey is doing his swaggering young man's shout. These are rawly exciting songs, but melodic, too, in the way that, say, Elvis Costello could be aggressive and tuneful at once. Plenty of them have affecting musical lines. Townshend at his best was always able to write tough songs that you might want to hum, and indeed the early Who, of the *Tommy* days and before, could sound at times a bit like a punk Beach Boys—think of songs like "I Can See for Miles," "The Kids Are Alright," "My Generation," "Substitute," "Pinball Wizard," "See Me, Feel Me." But those songs obeyed the dictates of genre, and were over after three or four minutes. On *Quadrophenia*, it is different. After a few verses and choruses, at exactly the moment where a traditional song would fade out, a space for improvisation opens up, and the players race into it.

The energy of the music has its counterpart in the lyrics. Townshend never wrote better words than here. The narrative of the "mod kid"—from teenage rebel to down-and-out, from London to Brighton, a boy both following the fashion and left behind by it—gives the lyrics shape and tautness. One of the sadnesses of being "trained" in English literature is that it makes you snobbish or uncertain about the literary quality of rock lyrics. When I was a teenager I used to think that Bruce Springsteen's phrase "the lonely cool before dawn" (from "Thunder Road") was great poetry. Nowadays, I still think it is pretty good rock writing, though a bit kitschy too, and to think thus is to have lost some essential trust. Townshend's writing can be pretentious, but at its best it is more sociologically acute even than Springsteen's, less flowery, and finely inclined to one-liners: "I was born with a plastic spoon in my mouth," from "Substitute"; "Hope I die before I get old," from "My Generation"; "Teenage wasteland," from "Baba O'Riley"; "And the parting on the left is now the parting on the right . . . Meet the new boss, same as the old boss," from "Won't Get Fooled Again."

There are scores of memorable lines on *Quadrophenia*. How about "Magically bored / On a quiet street corner," from "5:15"? Or the vicious male competitiveness—nowadays, it makes you think of hip-hop—of "Doctor Jimmy":

> *You say she's a virgin*
> *But, I'm gonna be the first in.*
> *Her fella's gonna kill me*
> *Oh, fucking will he . . .*

"Sea and Sand" is one of my favorite songs on the album. It starts almost bucolically, with the sound of seagulls, and an unaccompanied acoustic guitar.

But the rest of the band quickly tears that to bits, the acoustic is exchanged for taut, rhythmic slicings from Townshend on an electric guitar, Moon is loudly spilling himself round the kit, and we have instead a real raw rock song, a song that carries echoes of its 1960s roots in the English rhythm and blues of the mod club scene (think of Cream's "Crossroads," or early Stones) and also seems to peer forwards from 1973 to the English punk that is only a few years away—to one of Paul Weller's angry songs like "The Eton Rifles" or "Going Underground," or maybe something by Joe Jackson.

The reason that the seaside idyll has been shattered is that our young mod hero is not doing too well in Brighton. Drunk on gin, dreading his comedown from his drug-fed high, he is hearing voices (not one, not two, but four: "Schizophrenic? I'm bleeding Quadrophenic.") The song throws out a furious revolt:

> *Here by the sea and sand*
> *Nothing ever goes as planned*
> *I just couldn't face going home.*
> *It was just a drag on my own.*
> *They finally threw me out.*

One didn't have to have hypocritical or drunken parents (I didn't) to thrill, as a teenager, to the brutal exposure: "My mum got drunk on stout. / My dad couldn't stand on two feet / As he lectured about morality." The song doesn't really have a center, or even an obvious chorus; it opens out like a series of rooms, and then turns back on itself, as if the song's narrator were arguing with himself. There are four completely different musical refrains in the song—properly quadraphonic—and they are laid out in what one can later see is an A-B-C-B-D-A pattern; listening to the record, you just get a sense of powerful restlessness. After the tense opening, the sounds softens, and Daltrey's voice soars up: "The girl I love is a perfect dresser, / Wears every fashion, gets it to the tee. / Heavens above, I've got to match her. / I know just how she wants her man to be." But it turns out that mods don't really want to impress their girls so much as each other, and the desire to dress well turns defiant:

> *My jacket's gonna be cut slim and checked*
> *Maybe a touch of seersucker with an open neck*
> *I ride a GS scooter with my hair cut neat*
> *I wear my wartime coat in the wind and sleet.*

This is a verse that appears in an earlier song, and is repeated in this song as a way of binding the album thematically. It is a kind of soldier's marching refrain. It doesn't exactly exclude girls, but it belongs to the male gang, and returns us to that photograph of the young kid riding through London on his Vespa. You have a feeling that his bike means more to him than his lover. Then the song turns again, and the singer complains about not looking as good as the other guys—"So how come the other tickets look much better? / Without a penny to spend they dress to the letter"—finally ending with a verse that repeats the opening tune, and its anger and despair:

*I'm wet and I'm cold,*
*But thank God I ain't old.*
*Why didn't I say what I mean?*
*I should have split home at fifteen.*
*There's a story that the grass is so green.*
*What did I see?*
*Where have I been?*

"Thank God I ain't old." That was what the mod craze, which lasted from about 1962 to 1966, was all about, and why so many of the songs on *Quadrophenia* have to do with anti-parental rebellion. Pete Townshend's old flatmate, Richard Barnes, who came up with the band's name, has provided an excellent account of this world in his book *Mods!* (1979), essentially an album of old photographs with a long foreword. By the start of the 1960s, there was a generation of young British men newly liberated from some of the constraints of the previous decade. They were released from the obligation of national service in the army, they had jobs and no family commitments, and thus money to spare, and if they lacked immediate cash they could always buy stuff on hire purchase, recently inaugurated in order to get the consumer boom going. Mods had no time for the stifling popular music put out over the radio—the syrup served up by "entertainers" like Max Bygraves and Frank Ifield. They looked to America for music, and to Italy and France for fashion. Musicians like Townshend, Eric Clapton, Robert Plant, the Stones, the Animals, were deeply enamored of American blues and early Motown: Mose Allison, Marvin Gaye, James Brown.

These days, one tends to think of the '60s as a decade in which only near its end—when, say, the Beatles went long-haired and yogic, and when political rebellion announced itself explicitly—did the great rift become apparent that separated those born before and after the Second World War. But the mods were pioneers for the hippies, and had already declared an absolute break with their parents' values. In place of thrift and conformity and rectitude—the valucs that had helped win the war—they put decadence, rock music, and partying. They had their own bands, chief of which was the High Numbers, who later became the Who, and their own venues for live music, like the Marquee and the Scene in London, and the Aquarium ballroom in Brighton. They danced and took plenty of drugs, mainly amphetamines ("pills," "leapers," "uppers," "Purple Hearts"); Barnes reports that the Marquee had a big sign that read: "SPEED KILLS."

Despite the giddy air of revolt, mods were in many ways conservative. There was a Wildean streak to their decadence. Immense attention was paid to clothing and grooming. Italian suits, with short jackets and thin trousers with no turnups, were copied by English tailors. The jackets had to have side vents of at least three or four inches. Shoes were suede desert boots or long, pointed winklepickers. Hair, again French or Italian in cut, was kept short and neat—this was true of both girls and boys. The new coffee bars in Soho existed, in part, for peacock displays of the new fashions. Snobbery was very important. The Beatles, at least in their early years, did not make the cut. One of the reasons that mods so despised "rockers" was that they seemed aesthetically down-at-heel: they listened to pop music rather than rock, they wore their hair too long, and sported leathers and jeans. Scooters were favored over motorbikes because, says Richard Barnes, "unlike motorbikes, you didn't get oil on your clothes, or greasy hands."

The rivalry between mods and rockers became serious around the Easter Bank Holiday weekend of 1964. Groups of mods liked to ride from London on their scooters to the grim, drizzly resort towns on the South coast, like Brighton, Hastings, and Bournemouth. With nothing to do, they just hung around—"Magically bored / On a quiet street corner." Inevitably, there was minor vandalism, and scuffles with groups of rockers. A skirmish in Clacton, at Eastertime, was hysterically written up by the London newspapers as the decline and fall of civilization as we know it. Fights in Brighton and Margate, a few weeks later, were more serious. Windows were smashed, deckchairs hurled, and a policeman knocked unconscious. Newspapers showed a rocker lying facedown in the sand, while a mod kicked at his head. "There was Dad asleep in a deckchair and Mum making sandcastles with the children," wrote the tabloid *Daily Express*, "when the 1964 Boys took over the beaches at Margate and Brighton yesterday and smeared the traditional scene with more bloodshed and violence." The summer of 1964 was the summer of the beach riots. But mods and rockers found it very hard to define exactly which differences were worth fighting over. It was fighting in lieu of anything better to do. In several of the *Quadrophenia* songs, Townshend catches very well that excited collective aimlessness, the sense of being part of a long fuse looking for any suitable bomb. In "Bell Boy," the only song on the album sung by Keith Moon (who couldn't sing, and who basically growls a kind of stage cockney over his drums), our mod kid's friend, now employed at a hotel in Brighton, recalls being on the other side of the hotel door:

> *I'm newly born*
> *You should see me dressed up in my uniform*
> *I work in a hotel, all gilt and flash*
> *Remember the gaff where the doors we smashed?*

And in "Cut My Hair," the hero exults in his aggression:

> *Zoot suit, white jacket with side vents*
> *Five inches long*
> *I'm out on the street again*

*And I'm leaping along.*
*Dressed right, for a beach fight*
*But I just can't explain*
*Why that uncertain feeling*
*Is still here in my brain . . .*

That phrase "I just can't explain" sets off an echo of an early Who song that belonged to the early 1960s, "I Can't Explain." (Not being able to explain, not being willing to explain, is the great secret privilege of teenage rebellion; compare the Sex Pistols' sublime: "I don't know what I want, / But I know how to get it.") Looking back at the early 1960s from the early 1970s, *Quadrophenia* also inevitably looks back at the early career of the Who, since the mod explosion was inseparable from the Who explosion. *Quadrophenia* is by the Who and about the Who, if that does not sound too unbearably postmodern: at one moment in the album we hear a brief snatch of the old Who song "The Kids Are Alright." Townshend wrote a text, a kind of dramatic monologue, which is included with the book of *Quadrophenia* photographs, and intended as a commentary on them by the mod kid. In it, he tells us about his mum and dad, his drugs, his clothes, his final trip to Brighton, and his love of the Who:

*On the second night I saw the posters going up outside the Odeon for a WHO concert. I'd seen them down at Brighton. They were a mod group. Well, mods liked them. They weren't ex-*

*actly mods but mods did like them. They had a drummer who used to play with his arms waving about in the air like a lunatic. The singer was a tough looking bloke with really good clothes. If I hadn't have seen him near home I would have said his hair was gold. Real gold I mean, like gold paint. The guitar player was a skinny geezer with a big nose who twirled his arm like a windmill. He wrote some good songs about mods, but he didn't quite look like one. The bass player was a laugh. He never did anything. Nothing. He used to smile sometimes, but the smile would only last half a second then it would switch off again. My friend Dave said he smiled a lot more at his sister, they were engaged I think. His bass sounded like a bleeding VC10.*

Townshend is indeed a skinny geezer with a big nose; nowadays he is an old skinny geezer with a big nose. He has always been very good at dramatizing his sense of being an outsider, even when he is at the center of things, which is exactly the dynamic of *Quadrophenia*. The mod kid stands at the side of the road, watching the Who as they come out of their concert: "After the show I hung around outside waiting for them to come out. When they did they never bloody well recognized me. I shouted and one of them turned around and said 'How are you doing?' like he remembered me. 'Working?' he said. I hate it when people say that. Course I wasn't working. I was still at fucking school." The mod kid would like to be a "face" (the mod slang for a fashion leader), but is merely a face in the crowd, a wannabe musician. In one of the songs on the album, Townshend nicely nails this: "I got a Gibson (without a case) / But I can't get that even tanned look on my face."

There is generally thought to be something comical about remaining adolescent into gray adulthood. The aging rock star, still thrashing at his guitar, his bald head lightly beaded with sweat, and his clothes now unmentionably unfashionable, is a mocked figure. How much more comic, then, must be the person who has lived it all vicariously—the teenager who, having listened to *Quadrophenia*, went out onto the streets of his minor English town with a little more swagger in his gait, defiantly (but quietly!) murmuring "Dressed right, for a beach fight," and who, when he grew up, continued to enjoy that electricity of rebellion that surges through everything the Who played. Because I had a brother five years older than me, I was always too late for everything: I missed punk at the end of the '70s because I was still stuck in 1973. I have listened, on and off, to *Quadrophenia* since I was thirteen. But sometimes, now, at the age of forty-two, it feels strange to enter its world. *Quadrophenia* is itself a nostalgic album—it wants to be there, back on those beaches and in those Soho clubs of the 1960s. So when I listen to the album now, nostalgia is doubled, since I am looking back at my own youth, and also look back at the Who's youth, at an era when I was not even born. I become nostalgic for a rebellion I never experienced and for an

England I never knew. But if this seems merely touching, and even a bit silly, is it clear that conformity and "settling down," whatever that would mean, is the better alternative? Is it hypocritical to be old while also singing, "But thank God I ain't old"? I don't think so.

## JUST LIKE ME

The Jackson 5: *Greatest Hits* (Motown Records, 1971)
### Martha Southgate

The cover is almost as important to me as the album inside. The design is simple and memorable. The surrounding border is a dark blue, shot through with the fine crackling that age produces on old master paintings. Then an ornate filigreed frame of the sort found at the Metropolitan Museum. On the record jacket (but not on the CD insert), the edges of the frame around the photograph are perforated so that a girl can punch it out and hang the picture on her bedroom wall. But I never did that—I didn't want to disturb the pristine surface of the sleeve. Within the frame is a photograph of the Jackson 5 in all their big-Afroed, pre–plastic surgery, brown-skinned adolescent glory. They are wearing mock-Baroque costumes (though Tito is sporting his trademark newsboy cap—we called them "apple" caps in the '70s). They regard the camera unsmilingly—well, Jermaine has a sheepish half-smile—like the royalty they are. The crackling motif carries over lightly onto the photograph, reminding the viewer that there is mastery here, greatness embodied in five black boys from the rust-belt town of Gary, Indiana.

To a black girl from the rust-belt city of Cleveland, Ohio, the message was a powerful one. And that was before I even put the album on the turntable. My little sister and I shared a bedroom and I spent hours making up stories for her—and for myself, of course—about what might have happened the day of the photo shoot. Why Jermaine was smiling like that. Or how they'd been running late and their dad had been yelling at them and then they argued but then they calmed down for the picture. Or what funny thing Michael had said right before the shutter snapped. It seemed real to me. It seemed real to her. They were our brothers. They were our boyfriends. They were the best.

This album was not where my affair with the J5 started. Until they came along, my primary interest in owning pop music was limited to two albums that my mother had bought at the Salvation Army: *Distant Shores*, by Chad and Jeremy, and *Kicks*, by Paul Revere and the Raiders, which includes their cover of "(I Can't Get No) Satisfaction." (I was later surprised to learn that they weren't the first to record it. Who were these Rolling Stones guys anyway?) My horizons were ripe for some broadening. So in late 1969, when *Diana Ross Presents the Jackson 5*, their first album, came out, it was like a bomb had gone off. Hell, talk to any black woman who was between the ages of five and fourteen in the early 1970s and she probably had a similar experience. The J5 couldn't be denied. They were Motown's last great success story. By the time The Jackson 5's *Greatest Hits* was released in December 1971, they'd been going strong for two years. The album was simply a reaffirmation of (and further cashing in on) that success. They were everywhere, widely imitated but never duplicated by both white and black. (Remember "One Bad Apple" by the Osmonds? Or Foster Sylvers's "Misdemeanor"?) And I think we all know to whom every boy band, from New Edition to Hanson to the Backstreet Boys to 'N Sync and beyond, owes its musical DNA.

By late 1971, I was already a religious reader of *Right On!* magazine. There was a Jackson on the cover of every issue from January 1972 until April 1974. The J5 was the reason for the magazine's existence, but like so much else that was engendered by this band, the publication had greater significance. It was the first teen magazine with black teen idols, aimed at black teen girls. (I recently discovered that it is still published today, festooned with pix of the likes of Tyrese and Chris Brown.) But I didn't buy it for the history—I bought it for the boys. I used my allowance or the money I earned by having my brothers and sisters pay me to do their chores to buy as many issues as I could. I kept them under my mattress and treated them like holy relics, poring over stories like "Find Out What the J5 Are Really Like!!!!!" and completely fictional "typical" days in the life of the band, filled with mischief and fun. I believed every word of it.

I was an enthusiastic member of the J5 army. I'd worn my copy of their debut album thin. (I still have it; the cover is a mess.) I watched them every time they were on TV—on *Sonny and Cher*, on *American Bandstand*— and admired those charming, round faces, the awkward yet sharp faux-Temptations dance moves. But *Greatest Hits* was a special indulgence. It put all the good stuff in one neat package—no filler, no duds. And of course, there was that cover.

Ever since the massive success of "I Want You Back" in 1970, they had been unstoppable. They transcended race, they transcended age, they transcended every-thing. Every radio in America was swept away by that sound. And they could have lived down the street from me. Five regular black boys from Gary, Indiana—not that different from Cleveland, not that different from me or my sister or my brothers. How could I not love them?

Most of my girlfriends went for Michael, the cut-est, the most talented, the lead with the airy voice of an angel. Who could blame them? Listen to the author-ity with which this eleven-year-old—eleven!—sings Smokey Robinson's classic "Who's Lovin' You." Take the way he hits the first line—"When I had you here / I treated you bad and wrong, my dear." The longing for the sweet, now sadly lost, time of the "when" is palpa-ble as he toys with the word. He drags out the "bad"— "bahahad"—so that he has to artfully rush the final phrase. This isn't just fake *American Idol*–style playing with the notes. He *feels* it, in some nascent, unnameable way, and he makes sure that we feel it too.

I wouldn't have been able to say all this when I was nine or ten and Michael was eleven or twelve and I heard this song for the first time. But it gave me goose bumps. I know that. I listened to it over and over. I know that. And I know that all the girls in my fourth grade class spent lunch hour making up dance moves to J5 songs. My favorite move went with a line from "The Love You Save." The three sassiest girls in my class, Dena, Florida, and Shirley, would stick their preteen hips out and tap the wrists of their extended right arms with their left hands, where a watch would be, while singing, "Christopher discovered / You're way ahead of your time." Oh, how we loved them.

Though, if pressed, I would have had to admit that Michael was the most talented, my heart completely belonged to Jermaine, the middle brother and supposed bass guitarist (what you hear on the records is really Motown's crackerjack house band). I had a *Right On!* pinup of Jermaine smiling, alone against a blue background, that I can still envision as clearly as if I were looking at it right now. Back then I put enormous stock in the fact that his birthday was December 11, one day after mine. But, let's face it, he didn't stand out. You hear him occasionally. He's the one with the mid-range tenor in the call-and-response part of "I Want You Back," following up Michael's "All I need . . ." with ". . . Oh, is one more chance to show you that I love you" and alternating cries of "baby." To my knowledge, he only sang lead with the J5 one time, on a song called "I Found That Girl." His voice is fine, inoffensive. But it has none of the authority and dexterity of his younger brother's—perhaps that's why I loved it, loved him. I wasn't particularly authoritative or dexterous myself. I was short and shy and bespectacled. I was not one of the sassy girls tapping my arm as I danced. I was the one who sat and watched them in awe. I imagined that Jermaine would understand.

So I would sit with my friend Maren on the porch on sunny summer days, my orange Ball and Chain radio between us, and wait and wait and wait for the happy moment when the DJ at WJMO ("We Jam More Often") might deign to play "I Found That Girl." That moment almost never came around—though the song is on *Greatest Hits*, it was never truly one of their most popular. But Maren and I knew that if we didn't stay tuned, we might miss it. We might miss the moment when Jermaine's voice slid out of those tinny speakers and touched us. We could sit for a few hours in the service of that.

Some things I loved in my early adolescence—*Are You There God? It's Me, Margaret*, Barry Manilow, knickers—turn out to not be as good as I remember. But the exhilarating thing about the Jackson 5 is how good their best songs still are. In the course of writing this essay, I began to wonder what makes their music superior—I mean, nobody's still listening to "One Bad

Apple," you know? I wanted the thoughts of someone who writes and plays music, which, sadly, I do not. So I called my friend Douglas J. Cuomo, a guitarist and composer; once I got him going, we spent nearly forty-five minutes talking about "I Want You Back" alone. He gave me the language to articulate more precisely what makes their best songs work.

That thrilling piano riff at the beginning of the song—that's called a "gliss" (from *glissando*). It's accomplished when the pianist takes his thumb and runs it straight across the entire keyboard; it's a time-honored rock and pop technique, dating back to Jerry Lee Lewis and before. It starts the song out on an irresistible note of excitement and joy, the kind of thing that makes you shriek and skitter out onto the dance floor. Then the guitars chime in, a fairly complex bass line and a bouncy lead guitar riff that doesn't really change much. There are several inviting hooks throughout the song; every time one might start to feel rote, another one jumps in to reel the listener back in. Like the moment at the end of the second chorus when Michael sings "But now since I see you in his arms" and then the song cascades into a series of "uh-huh's" alternated with "all I want" and a distinct new hook in the bass line. It's as though you've been suspended on the edge of desire and suddenly, exquisitely, it's fulfilled.

Aside from the artistry of the music, there is that yearning, masterful vocal. Michael's voice is completely that of a child, yet it bears some of the assurance and wounded sorrow of a man who's been around and seen it all. A man who is longing for a purity that he cavalierly threw away.

Anyone who knows anything about the Jackson family knows that Michael in fact was living a life that a young boy shouldn't live, seeing things a young boy shouldn't see. When you look at his face now and consider the mess his life has become, it's apparent that the scars run deep, that the woundedness and longing that were so apparent in that boy's vocals had too much basis in reality.

And yet, somehow, the song is the sound of joy as well. The lyrics speak of loss, but somehow, you know that not only will he get that little girl back but that everything in your own life is gonna be just fine. And for those two minutes and fifty-eight seconds, it is.

Too bad it couldn't last. The Jacksons left Motown, acrimoniously. Their music deteriorated; they foundered. Michael, always the star, went out on his own and . . . well, we all know what happened to him. Who can forget *Thriller*? Who can forget his TV appearance on *Motown 25*? That moonwalk. That glove. That performance of "Billie Jean." Like the opening riff of "I Want You Back," it was a moment of pure pop perfection. But that moment, and the year or so that followed, were as good as it ever got for Michael. Looking at that footage now, you can see the seeds of destruction, as divine as the moment is. He's already had some plastic surgery—his typically African American nose has begun its long narrowing process, his cheeks are sharp-edged and bony. His hair is in a draggled, half-straightened Jheri curl—the height of fashion at the time, but already far away from the beautiful, natural, kinky hair he was born with. And those dance moves, so thrilling, would later ossify into something that looks as corny now as it looked glorious then.

When the J5 left Motown and entered their awkward adolescence, I entered mine, too. I began to leave them behind. I bought Jermaine's first solo record (called *Jermaine*) and I listened to it a lot, but if you'd forced me to tell the truth, I would have had to admit that it wasn't very good. I was riding an hour and a half away from my neighborhood every day to attend a predominantly white prep school. And I started to like "white" music—Eric Carmen and James Taylor and the Eagles and even Bruce Springsteen. The J5 became a bit of a dusty memory.

But I hung onto *Greatest Hits* then and I hang onto it still. I have it on vinyl, along with the original inner sleeve, which includes an offer to "Be Jermaine's Personal Soul-Mate!" This is a package of goodies that includes an ID card, sixty-five letter stickers, nine wallet-size photos, a "Giant" wall poster, and "Your very own Jermaine Jackson Personal Soul-Mate Poem Poster! Written for your wall by Jermaine himself!" (There is, of course, an identical offer for each Jackson.) I have the album on CD, replaced twice, once when it broke, once when my son lost it. And most recently, I downloaded it from my CD to my computer so I could listen to it while I wrote this essay.

When I was in high school, I thought I had to choose between "white" music and "black" music. Now, I know that division is ridiculous. Loving the Boss doesn't mean I have to reject the J5 or any of the soul music I also love. In fact, to reject their music is to reject a crucial part of myself—I didn't get that when I was younger. But thank God I get it now. For me, for any adolescent in the late '60s and early '70s in an all-black neighborhood in Cleveland (or anywhere else), the thing that was so important about the J5 was not only the delights of the music. It was how much like us they seemed to be. Back then, I imagined that their house in Gary was much like my house in Cleveland. Once I was an adult, I had the opportunity to visit Detroit's Motown Historical Museum, informally known as Hitsville USA. This gem of Americana is Berry Gordy's old home. It served as the original Motown studio, and since 1985, it and the house next door to it have formed a small, engagingly homegrown museum. I was enchanted by the degree to which Hitsville resembled the house I grew up in—only a little bigger, on the same kind of workingman's street in an all-black neighborhood, acoustic tiles in the basement like the kind my mom put up one year in our basement.

We know now that the Jackson family wasn't the happy clan they appeared to be—as it turned out, I was better off that my family wasn't really like theirs. And to this day, whenever I see yet another horrifying photograph of Michael, I wince. But nothing can take away the first clarion gliss of "I Want You Back." Nothing can take away the hours I spent talking with my sister about that cover photo on *Greatest Hits*. Nothing can take away the pride that those boys gave me, at a time when there weren't kids who looked like me out there to love and admire and dream over. There they were. There they were. And they were good.

Miaow: *Priceless Innuendo* (unreleased, 1988)
**Peter Terzian**

**A** bright late morning in early October, freshman year,
1985; there wouldn't be many more days like this. I had
been at college for only a few weeks. Two days before, I
had performed respectably on a French test, and it was
now time to go to another French seminar. I stepped
out of my dormitory onto the sidewalk, but instead of
turning left, the direction of the liberal arts building, I
turned right, toward the city. I would skip this one class,
I thought, and walk into Boston, to Newbury Comics,
a store famous for its selection of punk and new wave
records, and buy two albums that I had heard my new
friends talking about, the Smiths' *Hatful of Hollow* and
the Cure's *Head on the Door*. I spent a half hour or so
dawdling around the shop, looking over the display of
new releases, flipping my way through the alphabeti-

cally organized stock, savoring my freedom while batting back the unease and guilt that crept in at the edges. Afterward, I meandered around the Back Bay, carrying my new acquisitions in one of the shop's slippery square yellow bags, with its logo of a grinning, black-eyed cartoon face on the side. I imagined the students back in the classroom, while the pretty French teacher drilled away at parts of speech. Maybe I stopped somewhere to get a sandwich.

Thus began a rapid descent into not going to very many classes and spending a substantial portion of the generous hundred-dollar check my mother sent me each week on records. I ended up with a B minus in the French class. By the end of my sophomore year, my academic record was a shambles: a transcript sprinkled with Cs and a few Ds, a couple of incompletes that I would have to make up over the summer in classes that would cost my parents extra money, and the threat of having my scholarship revoked. My music collection, however, had grown exponentially. I had arrived at school with about twenty albums and a little box of cassettes, and over the next two years had filled two large dairy crates with records, bold and beautiful in their cardboard sleeves. I had formed a mental picture of the kind of guy I wanted to be, the kind I looked up to: the musical sage, with five, maybe six such full crates (records were always kept in crates, on the floor; you had to kneel to look through them), synapses firing with the titles of b-sides and production credits, the self-satisfied owner of out-of-print gatefold limited-edition singles and flexidiscs.

I was almost there. I was now buying a few albums a week, mostly from the dusty used record stores around campus. I would bring them back to my dorm room, play them once or twice, and then think of other records that I wanted. Sometimes I would sell a bunch back, but the economics of this didn't quite work out—the clerk would shuffle through a stack of ten albums, some of which he might have sold me the previous week, and then offer enough money to cover two new ones, which I would feel compelled to buy then and there. I sat in my room with all these records, and tried to read or study, but all I could think about was music. The melodies drifted around my head like clouds. I lay in bed, trying to fall asleep, my brain a jukebox that wouldn't shut off.

I could read and spell before I entered kindergarten, but I was never a deep or methodical student. My mind wandered. I got used to hearing the phrase "careless errors." One day, Miss Powers, my first grade teacher, gave us some worksheets to keep busy with while she led a small reading comprehension group at the long, low table at the back of the classroom. I squirmed in my seat, zipping through the exercises. When I finished, the other kids were still bent over their papers. I stood up and began to walk around the room on my own. It must have been autumn; I stopped to look over the display of dried foliage that we had all been instructed to collect, as though I were browsing the wares in a souk. Miss Powers called out to me over the heads of the children in her group. What did I think I was doing?

I needed to go back to my seat. Had I double-checked my answers?

I had, I lied.

I couldn't just get up and wander around as I pleased, she protested, incredulous.

But I was just looking at the leaves, I said.

Perhaps, Miss Powers told my parents I wasn't being challenged. In the middle of first grade, I was advanced into the middle of second. But then things began to slide. I was a speedy reader, tripping through book after book, but I couldn't get my math facts down. I looked out the window a lot. In class, the teacher's voice was reduced to a tiny Miss Othmar drone while I thought about the things I liked: amusement parks, stuffed animals, the Bicentennial. This pattern continued through grammar school—"Until Peter wants to put forth his own effort," my third grade teacher wrote on my report card, "there really isn't much we can do about it"—and into junior high and high school.

When I reached college, I thought maybe the clock would restart on my academic habits. But now there was no one to tell me to apply myself. No one cared if I showed up in class or not—not my professers, not my friends. And how much more interesting, I thought, what an education in *life*, to walk by the Charles River while listening to my Walkman, or to spend the morning in my room with my friend Tiger listening to records. Wasn't music teaching me things that I couldn't learn in class, I asked myself, about growing up, defying authority, developing a self? I hadn't found someone to love me—and I wasn't sure if that someone would be a boy or a girl—but I knew that when love came, I would have a thousand love songs under my belt to guide me through the experience.

My friends and I believed that there were two kinds of music. There was the kind that was played on the radio and MTV, the kind that ordinary people liked and that we sneered at. "Commercial," we called it: Mike + the Mechanics, the Outfield, things like that. And then there was the kind that we listened to, the kind that came out of punk and new wave and that seemed too unusual or threatening to be accepted by the larger world, but that fit our moodiness and our edginess, our endlessly shifting emotions, our tidal hipness. We had some difficulty naming this music. Alternative? Underground? College rock? Mostly, we looked to England, promised land of all things cool. We lay on our beds with the lights out, listening to the swoony, drifty Cocteau Twins, who sang, according to various reports, in Gaelic, or possibly in phonemes—either way, we imagined it sounded like angel wings being rubbed together. In an introductory philosophy class, I sat next to a girl with moussed blond hair and dangling hoop earrings who began talking to me when she saw the words "The Jesus and Mary Chain" written on the sole of my Converse High-Top. As we waited for the professor to arrive, she told me stories about her childhood. She was from a suburb outside of Boston and spoke in the city's signature accent. But she insisted that she had spent several years in London as a young girl. She had grown up on a street where the members of the Cure lived, she said, and sometimes they would play with her. I believed this; I would believe anything. My mumbly friend Bob owned every Smiths single, and masking-taped the sleeves to his walls in a grid. The tape wouldn't stick, though, and the covers took their turns falling to the floor. When I visited his room, he was usually standing on his bed, trying to make them all adhere at once, holding a sleeve in place with his elbow while attempting to construct a new masking tape loop.

I started dressing the part. A few weeks after my arrival at school, I had my left ear pierced. I started to button the top buttons of my shirts, which I now purchased at vintage clothing shops. I used hair gel. These seemingly random affectations were considered punky, but we didn't ask who it was that had decided this. It was as if some snickering older sibling had played a trick on us, convincing us that these absurd clothes were the height of fashion. But we treated our outfits as though they were secret signs; if you met another person dressed like you, you knew that you had encountered a potential friend, someone who would instinctively understand you. I believed that by shedding my crisp turquoise Ralph Lauren Polo shirts and donning a pilly, old mohair sweater with sleeves that fell over my hands, I had finally revealed my true self.

At some point during my manic record collecting I bought a compilation album titled *C86*. The British bands that I had so recently been introduced to—Siouxsie and the Banshees, Echo and the Bunnymen—were actually getting a little long in the tooth. Some of their songs were even making their way onto American radio, and they accordingly began adopting the glossier production values of the period. The two kinds of music, commercial and alternative, were getting mixed up. The purpose of *C86*, I think, was to wipe those older groups clean away. The twenty-two new and largely unheard groups on the compilation shared a rudimentary, lo-fi sound. The guitars were pretty and chiming or thick with feedback, accompanied by thudding drums; the lyrics were delivered in the speak-sing of childhood jump rope songs. The British music newspapers, the *New Musical Express* and the *Melody Maker*, came to label the bands "jangle pop" or "twee." The boys in the bands were slim, with pencil legs in dark jeans and floppy hair that fell into their eyes. The girls had sweet, round English faces; their hair, often dyed, flopped into their eyes too. Floppiness was the general aesthetic. The bands posed for publicity photos in boxy anorak raincoats—they were from England, after all.

Honestly, I wanted to like *C86* more than I did. A few of the songs—Primal Scream's bouncy "Velocity Girl," the Soup Dragons' punk-lite "Pleasantly Surprised," the Shop Assistants' gentle "It's Up to You"—stood out, and I played them for a while and then lost interest. The record would pave the way for a host of new British indie acts, but most of the *C86* groups (the title soon became shorthand for the genre) fizzled out within a couple of years.

But there was one song—side two, song three—that had little in common with the shoutier songs on the record. Rather, it sounded antique, like something you might hear coming out of the speaker of an old gramophone, the accompaniment to a jitterbug party on Jay Gatsby's lawn. The song was called "Sport Most Royal" and was by a band called Miaow, the British transliteration of what a cat says. The singer's voice was sultry and, at the same time, hummingbird-quick, so quick that I could barely make out the words—something about a place called "Hanson Farms" and a person named "Moses Malone."

Newbury Comics had two twelve-inch singles by the band in their bins. (These singles were pricier "imports," American labels of that era not being in the habit of releasing tiny print runs of records by unestablished British musicians with funny names.) One, "Belle Vue," had a red sleeve with a drawing of a parakeet wearing a dress. The disc had three songs, and was on a small indie label. The other, newer single, "When It All Comes Down," was on Factory Records, the high-cred label of Joy Division and New Order. The cover was a picture of a haloed, bearded holy figure carrying a palm frond and an upside-down hatchet—the kind of image that I might have seen on the mass cards that my grandmother collected. On the flip side of the sleeve was a photograph of the band in a wooded park. To this day, it's the only picture of the group that I've ever seen. Three serious young people clustered around a tree: a black man in a blazer and a striped baseball cap; another man, rather ominous looking, with a turned-up collar and close-cropped hair; and the singer, a beautiful, brooding, intriguing woman. Her hair was a mess of gold and black, and it flopped into her eyes. Her sleeves were rolled up to reveal the tattoo on her forearm: a cartoon of a cat with a top hat and a walking stick.

This is the hard part. How do I convince you of Miaow's greatness? Chances are that you've never heard them, or of them, but even if you have, I'm not sure you'd be sold on my claim. Cute, you might say, charming, but great? I've played Miaow for various friends over the years, and the responses have been, for the most part, politely interested but not thunderstruck. I made a tape for a work colleague in the late '90s—I was still listening to them regularly then, years after they had broken up. When I asked him what he thought, he shrugged and said, "Good indie pop." I've played them in my apartment and discreetly studied my boyfriend's face for any sort of reaction, a look of pleasant surprise, a "who's this?" Nothing. But he's often like that, preoccupied.

Since I can't play these records for you, I could try to capture the music in words. I could write about the high and husky vocal, which breathlessly trills the lyrics, breaking and bending the words into only semi-recognizable shapes, hiccupping, sighing, sometimes giving out a little yelp, like a puppy squealing in delighted play. I could write about the rubbery bass lines of Ron Caine and the marching-band drums of Chris Fenner and the snake-charmer horns and . . . I could do all that, but it would be useless—you'll just have to take my word for it that Miaow was one of the pinnacles of twentieth-century culture. Or not. Perhaps I'm wrong, and Miaow was just good indie pop. I can't tell, for my very soul seems forever bound to this music. I've lost all perspective. I hear the Beatles, I hear Bob Dylan, and I think, they're no Miaow. The first time that I spoke with Cath Carroll, the group's mysterious looking singer, on the telephone, I told her that Miaow was my favorite band of the 1980s. (I felt that I had to qualify my praise, and not say "of all time.") "Oh!" she said. "You've got problems." But I suspect that everyone is wrong, even Cath, and that I can hear something in these songs that no one else, or a very select few, can—a transmission from the heavens; a starman waiting in the sky. I listen to Miaow and I am convinced that for a short time, between 1985 and 1987, genius walked the earth in the guise of three musicians from Manchester.

But if I can't convince you that the songs of Miaow are as good as songs get, or even give an accurate description of what they sound like, perhaps I can explain how Miaow came to mean the world to me. It was now the summer before my junior year of college, and I had moved into an off-campus apartment, and I was, for the first time in my life, truly alone. I had passed two inauspicious years at school, and my future was uncertain. Though I didn't want to admit it, I missed my family. I sat in my new bedroom among my many compulsively collected records and stared out the window at the large empty park across the street. I made a tape of Miaow songs and played them on my Walkman as I moved aimlessly around the city. On the steps of the Public Library, the boy that I was seeing—the first boy who had ever asked me on a date, and whom I clung to for a few weeks before I began to feel claustrophobic—pulled my headphones off my ears to hear what was playing. "You listen to that song too much," he said.

The song was "When It all Comes Down," the apotheosis of Miaow's art, three and a half mountain-high minutes of yodels and handclaps that made my heart want to burst. Amid all this lovely hootenanny, I couldn't have told you what the song was about. But the title alone—well, in my own life, it was all coming down. I had come out to my parents, and my days were filled with long phone calls during which I tried to talk them through this unwelcome news. I kept picking up mundane jobs—at a cafe, in a housewares store, handing out shopping circulars in Harvard Square—and quitting them after a few weeks. I would make pancakes for dinner and leave the leftover batter in the refrigerator until it had turned green. I wasn't reading much or going to the movies. My school friends were mostly away for the summer, vacationing with families, doing internships. One afternoon my friend Alec, who was spending a few months working at a shaved ice stand on a Hawaiian island, called to ask how my summer was going. A spring inside me uncoiled, and I began to shake with sobs.

Miaow's lyrics were largely indecipherable, so I couldn't project too much of my sadness onto them. But twenty years later, when I first read the words of "Sport Most Royal" on Cath Carroll's Web site, I saw how relevant, in an oblique way, they actually might have been to my younger self. "Hanson Farms" was actually Hampstead Ponds, the two swimming holes, men's and women's, located on Hampstead Heath, a large natural park north of London; the ponds are popular summer hangouts for gay men and lesbians. The singer is celebrating her "flash girl"—they've "sprayed their names on every station southbound on the Northern Line" and they're "drinking Red Stripe by the water." I have no idea where my "Moses Malone" came from; the line is actually, "Close the closet door behind you, girl." Of course, I too was closing the closet door behind me, but with none of the reckless, hedonistic abandon of the song. Still, that abandon got through to me—what I heard coming out of my headphones that melancholy summer was the sound of pure joy.

In the fall, school began again. My friends came back to Boston. I had a new steady boyfriend, and my grades started to improve. I was reading more and studying diligently. I found Miaow's third single—"Break the Code," a seven-inch with the image of a ram, a tongue of flame emerging from its forehead, on the sleeve; oh, these enigmatic, enticing covers!—in an overlooked bin at the three-story Tower Records that had opened on Newbury Street. The band was already trying something new: "Break the Code" called up the rain-washed, nocturnal streets of a '40s detective movie, the guitar notes plucked out like Morse code, the keyboards emitting sinister car horns and cobra rattles.

Surely, I thought, an album would soon follow. These three singles must be the harbinger of a full release, ten or twelve new Miaow songs. Would they be as good, better? Would the album be released on an American label? Would that label make them change their name to "Meow"? Would there be a lyric sheet, so that I could finally make out the words?

I kept checking the "M" sections of record stores. Nothing. No mention in the new releases column of the *NME*. I asked the sullen record store employees if they had heard news of a Miaow album. They looked at me blankly.

A year later, no Miaow record had appeared. It was clear that the band was defunct; no new music was forthcoming.

I was always loving bands and leaving them. The Wolfgang Press, the Woodentops, Propaganda—I would spend long, immersive months with their music, proselytizing to friends, making mix tapes of their songs, and then within weeks I would move on to something new. By all rights, that's what should have happened with Miaow. But it didn't. Whoever was responsible for changing the records in my mental jukebox somehow overlooked the Miaow songs. Their few existing recordings stayed as vital to me as if I had just heard them for the first time. I played them, in my mind and on my stereo, over and over, for years. They were sustaining.

Playing these songs has not been easy. Miaow released three vinyl singles, each with one or two b-sides, in three years, as well as "Sport Most Royal"—a total of nine tracks. The band fell apart in 1988, and a few years after that, my turntable broke and I bought a CD player. I brought the singles to the home of a friend who could still play records and taped them, but then I wasn't happy with the quality of the tape. Even though it sounded fine, I thought it should be dubbed onto a more expensive cassette. I taped the first, just-okay tape onto the second, better tape—but the improvement in tape quality didn't mitigate the worrisome fact that the recording was now at a further remove from the original. Some years later, a friend with a CD burner made a disc of the nicer tape, which made the music more accessible, since by then cassette decks seemed to be going the way of turntables. The recording was now third generation, and didn't sound very good, but it was all I had to go on for a long while. It wasn't until 2002 that a digitally remastered disc of Miaow's collected works, also titled *When It All Comes Down*, appeared, the product of a small label that was reissuing music by Factory's lesser-known bands. The day I first held it in my hands may have been the happiest day of my musical life, if only in that it delivered me from all of the taping.

Still, listening to that compilation, it was difficult not to think of what might have been. Somehow history had taken a wrong turn. There should have been a Miaow album—two or three albums, in fact, an entire career. If not an exhausting, decades-long march, like their *C86* compatriots Primal Scream and the Wedding Present, then a blaze-of-glory run, five years in which they would have the chance to stamp the world with their sui generis sound. Was I asking for too much? What band doesn't even get one album? How many aren't worth three singles?

But there was, I found out later, a Miaow album. Sort of.

College ended. I stayed in Boston. I got one job, and then another. By the mid-'90s I was working at a publishing company. I sat in a cubicle, running sales reports in an outdated programming language that I would never master, and that often left me near tears. On my lunch break, I would walk to Waterstone's and stand at the magazine shelves, reading *Spin* and *Ray Gun* and *Puncture*—alternative rock had by then become mainstream rock. I dreamed about writing for these publications.

A few years before, Cath Carroll had put out a solo album on Factory Records, titled *England Made Me* after a Graham Greene novel. *England Made Me* wasn't the lost Miaow album, but it shared some of the same DNA. Half of the songs were recorded in São Paolo with Brazilian musicians, and their hectic polyrhythms were distant kin to Miaow's headlong guitar jangle. But other songs were lush and danceable, with percolating keyboard sounds; Cath's voice was cooler, more languid. I loved the album wholly, but in a different way than I loved Miaow.

I wasn't the only one who loved *England Made*

*Me*. Unrest, a D.C. indie band, wrote a tribute song called, simply, "Cath Carroll," and covered "When It All Comes Down" on an EP of songs by Factory bands. (They didn't know the words either, and more or less improvised.) Now I read in a magazine that a second Cath Carroll solo album would be appearing on Teenbeat Records, Unrest's American label. I found the label's e-mail address—a new thing—printed on the sleeve of one of their seven-inch singles. I wrote to ask if any magazine writers had approached them about writing a profile of Cath Carroll. No, they replied, not yet.

I will do this, I wrote back. I will be the one to interview her.

This was an incredible act of hubris, as I didn't know anything about writing a magazine story. I wasn't aware that you were supposed to "pitch" the idea; if an editor was interested, you set up an interview. Instead, I set up the interview first, figuring that I would go ahead and write an article and then send it to every music publication in America. Surely, somewhere, there would be a gruff but tenderhearted editor who would pull my neatly typed pages from their manila envelope, read them through, and say, "Not bad. Let's give this guy a chance."

A few weeks later, I had an hour-long telephone conversation with Cath, who, I discovered, was now a resident of Chicago; she had, in fact, moved there years earlier. I asked a lot of questions about her new album, but I was most eager to solve the mystery of Miaow. What had happened? Why did Miaow break up?

They fought, she said, and drifted apart, but not before writing songs for an album and recording demos in the living room of a band member's flat in South London. They planned to title the record *Priceless Innuendo*, a quote from one of the *Carry On* movies. (This was a series of cut-rate British comedies, set in a campground, a hospital, the army—wherever broad, saucy farce could be manufactured.) Factory Records even issued a catalog number. But their manager kept sending the demos back, telling them to try again. "He was probably right," she said. "There were a couple good ones in there, but some of it was just cringe bollocks." She couldn't remember who had the demo cassette. "I don't remember too much about that period," she murmured. She talked about Miaow as if it were just any other band, betraying no sense of its otherworldly specialness.

Over the next few weeks, I wrote my profile of Cath, organizing the paragraphs on index cards, typing draft upon draft, fussing endlessly over the words. When I was satisfied, I sent my finished version to a handful of music magazines—actually, my strategy was to send only the first page. I believed that this would tantalize the editors, and they would write back asking to see more. I didn't know that this was a sure sign of amateurism. Of course, I soon began to receive rejection letters, but I wasn't deterred. I sent another round of first pages to another batch of magazines.

I was sitting at my desk at work when I got a call from the editor of a small New York music magazine. He was a fan of Cath Carroll, he said, and he would be happy to accept my story. The magazine wasn't the most polished of publications—its layout looked only marginally better than my high school newspaper's— but it had a sincere, wide-eyed enthusiasm for indie music, and it ran articles by budding music writers hungry for a break. (I don't recall that money was a topic of discussion.)

I had never known such happiness. I told my friends. I told my parents. I didn't come up with ideas for other stories to write or other musicians to interview; I didn't think of this as a first step. I was simply happy that I had taken a step. I wanted to write about Cath Carroll and Miaow, and I had, and now the world would see.

But when I called a few weeks later to find out when the issue with my story would appear on newsstands, the editor told me that the magazine had run out of money and ceased publication. I could hear an echoey room on the other end of the line, the sound of boxes being packed.

I made many embarrassed apologies to Cath and her record label. She wrote back that she had liked my article—I had shown her the profile before it was to be published, another journalistic no-no—and asked if she might use some sentences for a press release. She promised to thank me in the liner notes for her next album. Needless to say, I was over the moon.

By the time that record came out, a few years later, I had become a writer. I had moved to New York City.

I took another do-nothing job at a publishing house, and spent my days trading with people in do-nothing jobs at record companies, books for compact discs. A friend introduced me to a magazine editor, who gave me an assignment, then another. I quit my publishing job and was eventually hired as an assistant editor at a magazine.

Cath and I kept in touch, first by letter, later by e-mail. Her messages were long, witty, and kind. We talked about our shared affections: London, Dusty Springfield, dogs and cats. We exchanged stories about our families. Every year around the holidays, I made a CD of my current favorite songs and sent it to all of my friends; one year I sent her a mix that had one of her own songs on it.

In one message, she mentioned that she had unearthed a tape with some old Miaow demo recordings. I begged her to make me a copy; she said she would be delighted. I kept a close eye on the mailbox, but the tape never arrived. After a few months, she wrote that she had listened to the songs and cringed. I didn't push the matter, but I thought about that tape for years, and how *Priceless Innuendo* kept eluding my grasp.

I can map out an alternate history. Imagine that *Priceless Innuendo* had made its way out of that South London flat, that the band had been sent into the studio, and that a finished, professionally recorded album had been released as intended in 1988. Say that the kink in the fabric of the universe was neatened, everything carried out according to plan. Would it have made my life any better?

I'd like to think so. On the simplest level, there would have been one more record in the world for me to love. But perhaps that would have been the problem—no matter how great it was, *Priceless Innuendo* would have been, in the end, one more album. Instead, I ended up with a mystery. I spent years scrabbling through books about Factory Records and post-punk and trawling indie music Web sites for any fact about the band that I could find, any mention of an unheard track. Strangely, there was pleasure to be found there.

Perhaps *Priceless Innuendo* affected me so much because it was not made. Life, in the end, is full of such lacunae. Miaow taught me that sometimes things just don't work out. Also, that there's a kind of beauty in the cracked porcelain. The complete recorded works of Miaow, as they are found on the *When It All Comes Down* compilation (which, by the way, has eight songs from John Peel radio sessions and two teasing tracks intended for *Priceless Innuendo*, and which, of course, I urge you to go out and buy), are perfect, whole.

It took me years to see that there was a kind of perfection in the cracked porcelain of my own life. In my thirties, I looked back at my underwhelming college record, the bad summers, and later, the dead-end jobs, the wasted dollars and hours. If I could start over, I thought, I would do everything differently. I spun out elaborate fantasies in which I was a conscientious student, landed a writing job just out of college, maybe wrote a book or two; traveled more, dressed better, handled my relationships with more care. Did everything right. A few years ago, I lay awake on a too-firm bed in a London hotel room, exhausted and strung out from jet lag. I tossed and turned in the air-conditioned pitch black, dredging up a lifetime of regret. Finally I shook my boyfriend out of his hard-won sleep. "It's all Miss Powers's fault," I said, bursting into tears. "She never should have suggested I skip a grade."

But there have been just as many moments when I realized that my life is rough and imperfect, but it's mine, no one else's. A day when you cut class to buy records shines in the memory in a way that a day when you dutifully go to class doesn't (though I sometimes wish my French were a little better). "I would have loved to have had your college experience," my therapist once said to me. "It sounds like it was a lot of fun." I was startled—I had never let myself think of it this way—but I had to agree that it was. There was a serendipity involved that I can't question. If I hadn't bought all those records, perhaps I would never have discovered Miaow. And if I hadn't discovered Miaow, perhaps I would never have become a writer.

Of course, the Internet changed everything. I've landed in an age when all the musical mysteries have been unraveled. Every out-of-print album and lost b-side, every demo track and unreleased alternate version that I've ever read about and thought I'd never get to hear has found its way onto my hard drive. Without much effort, I became the musical sage I so aspired to be.

After twenty years, the *Priceless Innuendo* demo tape has been unearthed once again, sonically spit-polished, and posted on Cath Carroll's MySpace page. A few months ago, I listened to the songs for the first time. Of course, music recorded in a living room onto a cassette tape will never have the sheen of music recorded in a studio. But the Miaow genius is there. Cath's pell-mell vocals are as lovely and thrushlike as ever, and the band is playing at its peak, branching out into flutey keyboards and steel drums and Latin rhythms that form a bridge to *England Made Me*. The tape is a rough sketch of a masterpiece—in this case, an unfinished masterpiece. I'm left wondering if these songs arrive too late or right on time.

# 20
## BEWIGGED

*Hedwig and the Angry Inch* Original Cast Recording
(Atlantic Records, 1999)
### Claire Dederer

Trilby and I are talking on the phone. Well, really, Trilby is talking. While she talks, I'm roasting a chicken for dinner. I seem to be always roasting a chicken these days. I butter the bird's skin, freckle it with paprika, and set it in the oven. It's an August afternoon, hot for Seattle. The kitchen window is propped open with a ruler. Outside in the backyard, my daughter plays in the sandbox while her baby brother whacks the apple tree with a stick.

Trilby is good at talking on the phone. Trilby is good at everything, including making friends. We met at a baby group a few years back when our daughters were infants. I liked her right off the bat. While the rest of the moms were muzzy with lack of sleep and uncertainty, Trilby was clear-spoken and clear-thinking. She even looked more in focus than the rest of us. Her skin was pink, her eyes a lucid brown, her hair a shiny black. She knew everything, including my own future. "We're going to be friends, Claire Dederer," she told me, and I felt lucky. Despite her apparent positivity, she possessed a goofy, contradictory self-doubt that rendered her deeply charming. "I'm such a loser," she'd sigh, as she was beset by the daily catastrophes of motherhood: the missed doctor's appointment, the unbrushed hair, the tantrum. She could tell you she made her own organic pureed yams for her daughter and somehow you didn't want to kill her.

Right now she is lobbying me to see a show with her: *Hedwig and the Angry Inch*. Trilby went last night with her sister. "It's a play about a drag queen," she tells me. "I swear it'll change your life."

I'm a little surprised by Trilby's invitation. It's not like her to go out two nights in the same week. It's not like her to go out at all. Trilby is a worker bee of family life. Like me, she has a small daughter, a baby son, a husband, and a job. She is not a barfly or a gadabout. She is a serious person, the kind of person who comes home from a full day at the university and makes bean soup from scratch while overseeing a wholesome craft activity for her children.

Even so, I don't want to see a play with her. "Didn't I ever tell you I hate theater?" I say. I feel sure I've told her this. It's one of those cranky refusals that make up the adult personality. I loathe everything about the theater: its stage makeup and its let's-pretend sets and its actors who, unlike movie stars, can look right back at you. "And drag queens," I add. "I hate them, too." With their gigantic lipsticked mouths and knobbly knees and plasticky hair, drag queens are simply theater in human form. That kind of self-aware showmanship just wears me out. Artifice, in short, is not for me.

"Look, Claire," Trilby says. "If you go with me tomorrow night, I'll buy your ticket, and you'll get a night off from making dinner and putting the kids to bed."

Which explains how, on a sticky August night, I find myself heading toward my idea of cultural molar extraction: a live theatrical show all about a drag queen. It's playing at a nightclub downtown. Trilby picks me up. She hasn't dressed for the occasion. She wears her usual retro print blouse, her usual corduroys, her usual pretty corkscrew curls. On the sidewalk outside the club, Trilby and I meet her friends Matthew and Sara. He plays guitar in an avant-garde noise band. She is a novelist. They terrify me.

We stand outside in line and make friendly conversation. We all have five-year-olds who will be starting at the same kindergarten in the fall. Only Trilby, with her genius for connection, would combine a drag show with a school parent get-together. The sun drops between the buildings to the west. Puget Sound is over there, probably starting to glow pink, but we can't see it.

Inside, the dance club has been reconfigured as a theater. Trilby, who normally struggles to finish a single glass of wine, goes to the bar to get us huge margaritas in plastic tumblers. She gazes distractedly around the room while she sips from her big cup, leaving Matthew and

Sara and me to cobble together our own awkward get-to-know-you chat. We are midway through a conversation about our mutual terror at sending our firstborns off to kindergarten when three scruffy-looking men climb upon the stage, pick up their instruments, and begin to bash their way into a rock song. This isn't what I was expecting. I was expecting the lame, not-quite-rock of contemporary musical theater. I was expecting uptight sub-rock. What I am getting is real—immediate and a little scary and very fast. I feel like that guy in those old Memorex ads that used to run in *Rolling Stone*. I am surprised my hair isn't blowing straight back.

And then a figure that can only be Hedwig strides onstage, dressed in red-white-and-blue hot pants, her yellow wig flipped back into a cartoon version of Farrah Fawcett's famous hairdo. She opens her giant red mouth and growls, "I was born on the other side / Of a town ripped in two / I made it over the great divide / Now I'm coming for you." She's not kidding, either. She's striding around the audience, sitting in laps, spilling drinks, gyrating against flustered men. She's coming for us. I look over at Trilby. She is literally perched on the edge of her seat, a huge smile on her face, clapping her hands together like a five-year-old at the circus. She may well be the single most delighted human being I've ever seen.

It's been a long time since I have been delighted by music. Listening to music was once a hugely important part of my life. Growing up, I had a lot of inchoate feelings and nowhere to put them, so I opened music like a giant box and dumped them there. I had Joni and Bob and Neil for love; Wire and the Fall for anger; Sonic Youth and Brian Eno for mystery; the charmingly homespun bands from the New Zealand indie label Flying Nun for friendship; Gram Parsons for sadness; and the Descendents for jokes. I was a snob. Anyone who would list the bands I've just listed is a snob. In a haphazard life of dead-end jobs and part-time studenthood, my snobbery was my organizing principle. Music was how I made sense of my days. I imagine I am not unlike you in this.

Then, maybe like you, I got a good job and a lovable mate and we had a baby and then another. My life got very crowded with people I actually cared about, work I wanted to excel at. And music suddenly was just . . . gone. There no longer seemed to be room for it in my life. I simply couldn't hear it. I'd crank up Wire's *Pink Flag* while I cleaned the house, or listen to the Belle and Sebastian CDs my neighbor burned for me, but the music never seemed to penetrate the woolly layers of my new life. It was like being dressed in a bear suit. I was enfolded so thickly that nothing got through. I missed music, but mine seemed a condition unimprovable by effort or intention. You couldn't force an aesthetic response. You couldn't will yourself to feeling.

I wonder now if I was missing the essential quality of a listener: a soul. The soul is heliotropic. It's a plant that grows in the light of what it wants. This heliotropism is a casualty of motherhood, which involves a lot of loading smaller plants into a car and driving them to wherever they happen to want to go. After a while of this, a mother grows so accustomed to having her desires stunted, or delayed, or ignored, she stops bothering to want anything. True, she continues to want the most important thing: that the kids turn out okay. But she stops wanting in the various, irrational way that is what uniquely defines her. She is too busy cooking dinner. Her faculty of desire—that is, her soul—grows atrophied.

So, there I am on a hot August night, a soulless roaster of chickens. When Hedwig comes for me, blond wig flying, I am in no way ready for her. I am sideswiped.

The structure of *Hedwig and the Angry Inch* is a story-within-a-story. Hedwig is performing her rock act for us; as she performs it, she tells us her own history in song and monologue. This sounds simple, but past and present loop each other so continuously that the play begins to resemble something composed by a Spirograph. As I watch, I try to keep track of the plot, but it's like listening to gossip about someone you've never met before. Hedwig begins life as Hansel, a little boy growing up on the wrong side of the Berlin Wall. When Hansel becomes a teenager, he acquires a suitor: an American GI whose best quality is that he gives away lots of candy. The GI has a plan. Hansel will undergo a sex change operation, marry the GI, and they will move to America. Hansel's Commie surgery, unsurprisingly, does not go as planned. Hence the play's central, unforgettable image: "My sex change operation was botched. . . . Now all I've got . . . is an angry inch."

Hansel, now Hedwig, follows her lover to America, where she ends up abandoned and alone in a trailer park. There's something about an affair with a rock star named Tommy Gnosis who rips off Hedwig's material. Meanwhile, her current husband, Yitzhak (who is played by a woman), glowers menacingly by her side. The whole thing hurtles toward a cathartic climax in which Hedwig appears before us almost naked and entirely wigless.

The play's deep eccentricity reminds me of something, and finally I put my finger on it: *The Nutcracker.* *Hedwig* and *The Nutcracker* share a quality of dreamy unreality. Both plays exist inside a strange, sealed universe. Both are irrational if looked at from the outside, but possess an interior logic and sanity if you just climb inside and believe absolutely everything that's thrown at you. Both present fully formed mythologies of characters who are not only unknown, but because of their essential fluidity, are impossible ever to know.

Also, like *The Nutcracker, Hedwig* is really all about the hits. Hedwig stomps around the stage in her knee-high boots and her sequins and her hot pants, and that's how her songs come across, too: tarted up. As I discovered during those opening chords of the show, this is undeniably rock music. But it's rock music as imagined by drama geeks. It's rock music in a wig. Every song crescendos. Every song emotes wildly. Every song exhausts every possibility. To my sheepish surprise, I am carried away by all the spangled emotion. Maybe my too-cool (if highly out-of-date) record collection is just that: too cool. Maybe painted-up, red-mouthed, big-top artifice is just what I've been missing.

I glance down the aisle past Trilby. Sara and Matthew, effortlessly chic in sideburns (him) and vintage tee (her), are sitting there like the personification of my old snobberies. (I will find out later they are possibly the sweetest couple ever.) I start to wish it were darker in the room. I start to wish there were no witnesses. I want to get lost in all that overheated music.

I can hear influences everywhere, always beginning and ending with the polestar of David Bowie. The show climaxes with "Midnight Radio," an anthem sung in the lonesome, nostalgic, last-man-on-earth yowl that Bowie perfected in songs like "Drive-In Saturday." But even as my mind is shuffling through piles of old albums, isolating and identifying influences and musical jokes, the song is seizing me. "Midnight Radio" spoofs the whole notion of a massive rock anthem, and grips me as powerfully as any anthem ever has. It's doing its job—the production of emotion in the listener—perfectly. I don't even know what emotion I'm experiencing: It could be love, it could be pain. It's an undifferentiated mass of feeling. "Lift up your hands," sings Hedwig, as the song rises to its crescendo. "Lift up your hands."

Trilby, neatly pretty in her blouse and her curls, is on her feet, waving her arms in the air, singing along, and I think I see tears shining on her cheeks. I let my old snobberies slip away. I try not to worry what Matthew and Sara will think. And I stand up too.

• • •

The show ends. We linger on the sidewalk outside. Sometimes, on a hot summer night, a city can feel like the center of the world. Sometimes a city can feel like a cataract, into which everything, everything is pouring. I haven't had the feeling in a long time. But I have it now. We stand under the night sky for a few moments with the rest of the stragglers. Then we get into Trilby's Honda and drive home. The kids will be up early tomorrow morning.

Trilby appears at my house the next day with a copy of the cast recording. We have tea, then she's off again. There's a whole city of people just waiting to be introduced to Hedwig! She calls me a few hours later to check up on me. Have I noticed the background harmonizing on the line "tits of clay" at the end of the song "Angry Inch"? Did I know that the lyrics to "The Origin of Love" are based on Plato's philosophy of love? Have I listened—no, really *listened*—to "Wig in a Box"?

Over the next few weeks, I watch as my sensible friend is caught in the grip of an obsession. She can talk of nothing else. She leaves her husband and kids at home and goes to the show again and again and again. With typical diligence, she learns the genesis of the piece. The character of Hedwig was developed by the writer and actor John Cameron Mitchell at a series of performances at the New York club SqueezeBox in the '90s. Eventually these shows gave rise to an Off-Broadway play, and then to a film. Trilby and I duly rent the film and watch it gobsmacked, mesmerized by

Mitchell, whom we regard with a kind of awe: he is the source. Like true connoisseurs, we appreciate the lesser-known players as well, including Mitchell's lyricist and composer, Stephen Trask, whom we consider wildly sexy. We watch the DVD extras over and over, learning the Hedwig creation myth. We meanwhile harbor in our breasts a friendlier kind of love for our local Hedwig, the cherub-faced, oddly menacing actor Nick Garrison.

Trilby's enthusiasm seems to fan my own. I spend August careening around in my VW van, driving the kids to swim lessons and playdates, singing along to the cast recording. I love the feeling of having Hedwig, in all her ridiculous, bewigged pain and pathos, going through my days alongside me. When I unload the kids at their destination, my eyes are red, sometimes from crying, sometimes from laughing. Trilby and I do our chores, meet our deadlines, feed our children, but we exist simultaneously in a mental landscape that is as rococo and mannered and artificial as the court of Marie Antoinette. I can't tell you what a relief it is.

If you stripped your life down to a list of responsibilities, if you only did the things that needed to be done, what would happen to you? What would you become? I don't know the name for the sickness that comes from too much reality, but I do know its cure: music, and friendship, and artifice.

Trilby and I get babysitters and take our husbands to the show's closing night. Our husbands are tall, dark, quiet men, and as they watch, they neither weep nor sing. But they seem to enjoy both the show itself and their wives' manic, teary-eyed, somewhat hysterical response. This time, I notice that Trilby and I are not the only women in the room who are pushing forty. True, the audience is mostly comprised of drag queens and hipster boys. But sprinkled among them are women. Some in night-on-the-town dresses, some in Hedwig-inspired wigs, some in sweatshirts spattered with what looks suspiciously like baby spit-up. The women are laughing and singing and crying. The women are standing up. The women are lifting their hands in the air.

# CONTRIBUTORS

**CLIFFORD CHASE** is the author of the novel *Winkie*, which was an *Entertainment Weekly* Must-Read, a *New York Times* Notable Book, and a finalist for a Borders Original Voices Award; the book has been translated into eleven languages. He is also the author of a memoir, *The Hurry-Up Song*, and editor of the anthology *Queer 13: Lesbian and Gay Writers Recall Seventh Grade*. He lives in Brooklyn.

**KATE CHRISTENSEN**'s was the recipient of the 2008 PEN/ Faulkner Award for her fourth novel *The Great Man*. She is also the author of *In the Drink*, *Jeremy Thrane*, *The Epicure's Lament*, and most recent, *Trouble*. Her stories, reviews, and essays have appeared in a variety of publications, including *Elle*, *Real Simple*, *Tin House*, Salon.com, and many anthologies. She has sung and/or played viola in a variety of classical ensembles and bands. She lives in Brooklyn.

**STACEY D'ERASMO** is the author of the novels *Tea*, which was a 2000 *New York Times* Notable Book; *A Seahorse Year*, which won both a 2004 Lambda Literary Award and a Ferro-Grumley Award; and *The Sky Below*. She was a Stegner Fellow in Fiction from 1995 to 1997. Her essays, features, and reviews have appeared in the *New York Times Magazine*, the *New York Times Book Review*, and *Ploughshares*. She is an assistant professor of writing at Columbia University.

**ALICE ELLIOTT DARK** has published three books of fiction, *Naked to the Waist*, *In the Gloaming*, and *Think of England*, and many essays. She teaches at Rutgers-Newark, where she's Writer-in-Residence in the MFA program.

**CLAIRE DEDERER** writes about culture for the *New York Times* and other publications. Her first book, *Poser: A Memoir in Twenty-four Yoga Poses*, will be published by Farrar, Straus and Giroux. In 1992 she cowrote, with Trish and Victoria, an absolutely filthy song titled "The Nasty Masty," set to the tune of the Sex Pistols' "The Great Rock 'n' Roll Swindle." It was performed once, by the Presidents of the United States of America, at the Crocodile Café in Seattle. It is really too dirty to quote here.

**LISA DIERBECK** is the author of the novel *One Pill Makes You Smaller*, a 2003 *New York Times* Notable Book. A two-time Pushcart Prize nominee, she has written for such periodicals as the *Boston Globe*, *Elle*, *Glamour*, the *New York Observer*, the *New York Times Book Review*, *People*, *Time Out New York*, and *O, The Oprah Magazine*. Her nonfiction is featured in *O's Guide to Life: The Best of O, The Oprah Magazine*. She lives in Brooklyn.

**JOSHUA FERRIS** is the author of the novel *Then We Came to the End*, a National Book Award finalist and the winner of the 2007 PEN/Hemingway Award. His second novel, *The Unnamed*, will be published in 2010.

**MARK GREIF** is a founder and editor of *n+1*. His writing has appeared in the *London Review of Books*, the *New York Times*, and *Harper's Magazine*, and has been anthologized in *The Best American Essays* of 2005 and 2007.

**DANIEL HANDLER** is the author of three novels under his own name and at least sixteen under someone else's. He has served as the adjunct accordionist for the Magnetic Fields, among other pop efforts.

**JOHN HASKELL** is the author of a short story collection, *I Am Not Jackson Pollock*, as well as two novels, *American Purgatorio* and, most recently, *Out of My Skin*. His stories and essays have appeared on the radio programs *The Next Big Thing* and *Studio 360*, and have been published in *The Show I'll Never Forget*; *The Best American Nonrequired Reading*; *Yours in Food, John Baldessari*; and *All the More Real*, among other books. He has contributed to a number of magazines, including *Black Clock*, *A Public Space*, *n+1*, *Conjunctions*, *McSweeney's*, and the *Believer*. His work has been translated into more than ten languages.

**SHEILA HETI** is the author of the novel *Ticknor* and the story collection *The Middle Stories*. She collaborates frequently with other people.

**BENJAMIN KUNKEL** is the author of the novel *Indecision* and one of the founding editors of *n+1*.

**PANKAJ MISHRA** is the author of the novel *The Romantics*, and the nonfiction books *An End to Suffering: The Buddha in the World* and *Temptations of the West: How to Be Modern in India, Pakistan, Tibet, and Beyond*. He tried to learn the sitar but happily realized, early on, that he had no musical talent.

**TODD PRUZAN** is a longtime magazine editor. His book *The Clumsiest People in Europe*, an anthology of nasty geography books by the Victorian children's writer Favell Lee Mortimer, came out in 2005. He lives in New York with his wife and daughter.

**ASALI SOLOMON** was born and raised in West Philadelphia. Her first book, a collection of stories entitled *Get Down*, was selected as one of the National Book Foundation's "5 Under 35" in 2007. She has also received the Rona Jaffe Foundation Writers' Award. Solomon's work has been featured in *Vibe*, *Essence*, and the anthology *Naked: Black Women Bare All About Their Skin, Hair, Hips, Lips, and Other Parts*. She is at work on *Disgruntled*, a novel about people who hate their jobs, but what she most hates are R & B pop songs about strippers.

**MARTHA SOUTHGATE** is the author of the novels *Third Girl from the Left* and *The Fall of Rome*. She is working on a third novel, which will be published by Algonquin

Books. Her essay "Writers Like Me" appeared in *The Best African American Essays* (2007). She has received fellowships from the Bread Loaf Writers' Conference, the MacDowell Colony, and the Virginia Center for the Creative Arts. She lives in Brooklyn with her husband and two children. You can visit her Web site at www.marthasouthgate.com.

**JOHN JEREMIAH SULLIVAN** was born in Louisville, Kentucky, and now lives in Wilmington, North Carolina. He's a correspondent for *GQ* and a contributing editor at *Harper's Magazine*. He's been the recipient of a Whiting Writers' Award, a National Magazine Award, and a research fellowship at the New York Public Library's Cullman Center for Scholars and Writers. His essays have appeared in the *Best American Magazine* and *Best Music Writing* collections, as well as *The Oxford American Book of Great Music Writing*. His first book, *Blood Horses: Notes of a Sportswriter's Son*, was named a Book of the Year by *The Economist*. He once got on eBay and bought a pre-CBS Fender Duo-Sonic with the original, naturally distressed, lipstick-red paint job. On it he often plays unrecognizable fake-book versions of country blues classics.

**COLM TÓIBÍN** is the author of five novels, including *The Blackwater Lightship* and *The Master*; a volume of short stories, *Mothers and Sons*; and a number of travel books, including *Homage to Barcelona*. His work has been translated into twenty-five languages. He is a regular contributor to the *London Review of Books* and the *New York Review of Books*, and has been a visiting writer at the University of Texas at Austin, Stanford University, and Princeton University.

**JAMES WOOD** was born in 1965, in Durham, England, and educated at Cambridge University. He worked on the books pages of the *Guardian*, in London, for several years, before moving to the United States in 1995, where he became a senior editor at the *New Republic*, in Washington, D.C. He has been a staff writer at the *New Yorker* since 2007, and is the author of a novel (*The Book Against God*), two books of essays (*The Broken Estate* and *The Irresponsible Self*), and a book of literary criticism (*How Fiction Works*).

# ACKNOWLEDGMENTS

This anthology would not have been possible without the unfailing patience and support of my agent, Anna Stein, and my editor, Rakesh Satyal.

Lexy Bloom, Rob Crawford, David Doernberg, Sean Howe, Christine Kenneally, Patrick Nolan, Shelly Petnov-Sherman, Lorin Stein, and my parents, Richard and Barbara Terzian, helped in countless ways. Stacey D'Erasmo generously assisted with the proposal. Thanks to Caleb Crain, for his love and encouragement.